Openings to Renewal

Peter J Cullinane

ATF THEOLOGY

Adelaide
2011

Vatican II Series

Openings to Renewal

Letters to the Church

Peter J Cullinane

Cover design by Astrid Sengkey
Illustrations by Fitzbeck Creative, Wellington, NZ.

ATF THEOLOGY

An imprint of the ATF Ltd
PO Box 504
Hindmarsh, SA 5007
ABN 90 116 359 963
www.atfpress.com

Dedicated to Pope Paul VI

to whom was entrusted the helm

where the river meets the sea.

Table of Contents

Foreword

Cardinal TS Williams DD

Renewal must be first and foremost *the work of the Holy Spirit.* In his opening message to the Second Vatican Council, Pope John XXIII said

> We are lacking in human resources and earthly power. Yet we lodge our trust in the power of God's Spirit who was promised to the Church by the Lord Jesus Christ.

In line with that reminder, every session of the Council and every meeting of its Commissions commenced with the prayer 'Adsumus' composed by St Isidore of Seville in 619:

> We are here before you, Holy Spirit . . .
> come to us, remain with us,
> and enlighten our hearts.
> Give us light and strength to know your will,
> to make it our own, and to live it in our lives . . .
> Unite us in the bond of love,
> and keep us faithful to all that is true.

The pope also identified a second crucial element of renewal: it is *impelled by the love of Christ*:

> As we undertake our work, therefore, we would emphasise whatever concerns human dignity, whatever contributes to genuine community of peoples. 'Christ's love impels us' (2 Cor 5:14) . . .

Renewal impelled by the love of Christ and the power of the Holy Spirit is *undertaken in joy and hope*—sure signs of the Holy Spirit. The poem by the Jesuit, Gerard Manly Hopkins, known by its opening line 'The world is charged with the grandeur of God', expresses in its final lines the source of the Church's joy and hope:

> There lies the dearest freshness deep down things . . .
> Because the Holy Spirit over the bent world
> broods with warm breast
> and with ah, bright wings.

Renewal enlivened by hope and joy strikes out in new directions, explores new pastoral approaches, confronts with new initiatives the problems emerging in a rapidly changing world. A return to pre-conciliar methods will not respond adequately to today's challenges and difficulties. Renewal is impeded when it is mistaken for novelty. It is hampered by less than willing acceptance of the dictum *Ecclesia semper reformanda*. It is rendered impotent when maintenance is preferred to mission.

John XXIII challenged the Church to open the windows and let the breath of the Holy Spirit blow through. But now, as then, some see in the refreshing, invigorating, liberating breath danger of a destructive hurricane, and plead not only for the windows to be closed, but for the shutters to be secured as well. Their nostalgia for the past can be so pervasive that it drains them of all energy and enthusiasm, diminishing their ability to serve the Church of here and now.

Renewal doesn't require a 'new programme'. As Pope John Paul II insisted in his Apostolic Letter *Novo Millennio Ineunte* 2001:

> The programme already exists: it is the plan found in the Gospel and in the living Tradition, it is the same as ever. This is a programme which does not change with the shifts of times and cultures, even though it takes account of time and culture for the sake of true dialogue and effective communication.

Bishop Peter Cullinane's book explores the implications of this. He is well qualified to do so from his thirty years of episcopal ministry, not only serving his own diocese, but also representing the New Zealand Catholic Bishops' Conference in a number of areas central to the mission of the Church. Together with his fellow bishops he has taken part in four 'Ad Limina Apostolorum' visits to meet with the Holy Father and with officials of the Vatican Dicasteries, and has taken part in two Synods of Bishops.

Careful scholarship, pastoral sensitivity and compassion permeate each Letter. There is no one responsible for pastoral care in parish or chaplaincy who could not profit from the analyses, explanations and insights contained in each 'opening to renewal' discussed by Bishop Cullinane. It would not be out of place for some of these letters to be issued as pastoral letters intended for every parishioner, and for some to be addressed to Synods of Bishops.

Readers, whatever their roles in the Church and its renewal, through study of these Letters, will be encouraged to contribute to warm, inclusive and collaborative community, wholeheartedly and joyful celebration of Mass and sacraments, ready willingness to open themselves to growth and transformation, eagerness to serve those in need, enthusiasm to proclaim the good news of redemption, and readiness to witness to their faith by the manner of their lives, their efforts to advance Church unity, and their concern to build a just society.

Preface

These are not letters previously sent to individuals and now being brought together. They were written for this book. I have called them 'letters' instead of chapters to allow for their different lengths and the different levels of scholarship required by each topic. It also allows for a more personal style of writing.

I have chosen a few topics relevant to renewal, and my comments are limited to how they open up opportunities for renewal, or illustrate the ongoing need for it.

But renewal is not primarily about topics and issues, as some so tediously seem to think. Those who think the Church would be stronger if it changed some of its teachings don't seem to take seriously enough the experience of those churches that have already changed those same teachings.

The Church, and therefore its renewal, are part of the mystery of God's grace at work in the world. Yes, the issues matter, but how we address them depends on how radically we open ourselves to God in our own continuing conversion, contemplation and compassion.

Add to that: co-responsibility—the shared responsibility of all of us for the Church and its mission in the world. This in turn requires transparency and genuine dialogue at all levels. These letters are offered as part of that.

P J Cullinane
Bishop of Palmerston North
New Zealand

Letter One

In The Midst of Weakness—A Time of Grace

Dear Theophilus,

Much water has flowed down the Orontes since Luke wrote to you recording the Acts of the Apostles. Those were heady days. Didn't we catch a glimpse of that excitement ourselves after the Second Vatican Council? Sometimes, though, I wonder whether Luke, Barnabas and Paul would recognise us…

I know well the sacrifices that Catholics have made for the faith down to our own day. Now, with sad hearts many have seen their own children walk away from it, some of them in search of God elsewhere! What is that saying to us?

Ancient wisdom has it that the Church is always to be reformed (*ecclesia semper reformanda*)—always called to be more faithful to the gospel. That is what I mean by 'renewal' in this letter. Love and loyalty require it.

I have had the privilege of living on both sides of the Second Vatican Council. I was formed by the Church of the 1940s and 50s, and I am grateful to it. I know its mindset intimately. But my thirty years as the bishop of a diocese (in New Zealand) and as a member of the universal College of Bishops have been since the Council, and from this vantage point I recognise why Vatican II was so necessary.

Yet forty five years after the Council's conclusion, there are still some who need assurance that it was necessary, and others who need to be assured that the hope it gave them was not, and will not, be in vain.

I write to support those who still share Pope John XXIII's vision for the Church, and who need to know that it is still a work in progress. A Church that is too routinised and over-institutionalised does not evangelise. Pope John XXIII's image of opening the Church's windows for fresh air comes to mind when we recognise freshness in the way the Spirit is moving today, especially among young people. (See also Pope John Paul II, *On Entering the New Millennium*, 9.)

I am thinking, too, of those who hanker for a Church they never knew, and who therefore do not know why the Council needed to happen; and others who do remember how it was and fear that we have 'lost something.'

I write for all who need to better understand the underpinnings of renewal, the core principles that give coherence to what otherwise appear only to be 'changes'. And for those who need to know that 'continuity' involves more than ecclesiastical traditions. It is about being *radically faithful to the Gospel*, no matter what that costs the Church.

I am addressing those on the one hand who think the Council was a 'mistake', as well as those on the other hand who have slipped, more than they realise, into merely political, or even secular, ways of judging the Church. The merely liberal agenda falls short of what is required for radical renewal, which is about conversion, contemplation and compassion.

At the same time, the Church is not served well by those who too conveniently brand all criticism as disloyalty. They have not yet learned lessons from the Church's own history. Respectful dialogue is normal in a healthy Church, and that requires transparency.

I write to suggest that a *deeper acceptance* of the Second Vatican Council would create more common ground between the generation that 'grew up within a strong Catholic culture and to some extent reacted against it, seeing it as overly stifling and controlling' and a more recent generation that has grown up in a 'rootless secular culture' and so feels the need for a strong sense of Catholic identity, and is less uncomfortable with more traditional ways (John L Allen's apt description).

I write also for those who intuit that renewal of the Church is too small a concern and too narrow; that God is thinking of the *world*, and that 'what is needed is for the Church to be what it is meant to be, a living model of renewed social relationships depending upon renewed relationship with God' (Archbishop Rowan Williams, quoted by Theo Hobson, in *Anarchy, Church and Utopia*, [London: DLT 2005, 18].

Throughout these letters I am presupposing that the Church is an on-going creation of the Holy Spirit whose action within this community becomes a sign of God's saving purpose for all, unfolding within human history.[1] Renewal enables the Church to be more clearly that kind of sign.

I am writing for those who think that renewal takes place somewhere out of their reach while they themselves feel left out of helping it to happen. I want them to know how much it depends on them.

These letters are for those who still believe renewal is worth making sacrifices for, and who might yet see it as their role to reach out to those who do not. We can re-discover the faith ourselves when helping others to re-discover it.

I believe this is a time of grace, and that God is most at work in our weakness. The renewal of the Church is not the same as success as we usually understand it—fortunately. Rather, it is an experience of grace and divine mercy.

This was the point of a meditation by Cardinal Godfried Danneels given at Lourdes in October 1996. He saw the Church of today in a kind of exile. He was reminded of the exile of the Hebrew people to Babylon, which they had largely brought upon themselves—a kind of iconic exile. From their experience of finding themselves despoiled, bereft and humiliated they were to learn that salvation does not come from our achievements, but from the undeserved, abundant gift of God's mercy.

1. See Dogmatic Constitution on the Church (*Lumen Gentium*, 1964) (LG 48); Decree on the Church's Missionary Activity (*Ad Gentes*, 1965) (*AG*) 1.

At the height of its power, Israel could only conceive of God as a valiant warrior, whereas in exile Isaiah wrote his most beautiful passages on the maternal gentleness and compassion of God.

During the 1950s, the Church too seemed to be at the height of success and achievement with its full seminaries, full convents, full pews, its influence and prestige. Something needed to happen to shake us out of 'the myth of spiritual and ecclesial self-sufficiency' (Danneels). Like God's people throughout salvation history, we learn through our own experience of failure and unfaithfulness that salvation is not within our own power; it is pure gift and mercy (Eph 2:4–10).

Some lament as did Daniel in his day that 'we have no temples, no offerings, no sacrifices, no priests. . . ' (Dn 3:38). But it just too easy to blame the Second Vatican Council for that. Like Daniel, we might well confess that we have sinned and betrayed our trust. But in the midst of this true prophets recognise a time of grace. [2]

For the Church, as for our selves, renewal is the power of God at work in those who know the experience of weakness. What Michael Buckley SJ said in his memorable letter to young Jesuits on the vigil of their ordination about the grace that comes from being 'beset with weakness' (Hebrews) applies equally to the Church:

> Weakness . . . is the night in which the Lord appears—not always as self-reassurance, but more often as a power to continue faithful even when we do not feel the strength. . . It is this night, and the heavy work of rowing against the storm and threatening waves, that bring him to us (*Because Beset by Weakness,* www.nysj.org).

Some came to Jesus who were sure of themselves. The blind and the lame, however, came sure only of Him. And they were made new.

---

2. It is not unlike the way as individuals we come to experience Hope. Psalms and saints alike speak of experiences of darkness, desolation, despair and even damnation. It is when we have no foothold of our own left, and our situation is impossible, that we really place our hope in God *alone*—for whom nothing is impossible. Then, in God's time, we experience being lifted up in a way that is different from all our striving. Our 'thank you' is made of the same deep inner conviction that, yes, in the end, 'all will be well'. We give thanks in advance, and can live with the unanswered questions. Hope changes everything even before anything has changed.

Letter Two

'Making All Things New'

Dear Patrick,

We met in Rome when I was a student priest. You had been a leader in Joseph (later Cardinal) Cardijn's Young Christian Workers' Movement, and if I remember rightly you were in Rome to meet with Monsignor Pietro Pavan who was working on what became Pope John XXIII's Encyclical *Peace on Earth* (*Pacem in Terris*, 1963) (*PT*).

Pope John was aware of a cleavage between how people thought of religious faith and how they thought of the rest of life. Religious faith had come to be perceived as a kind of 'add-on' to the rest of life—something we can take or leave and not miss; not really integral to human life itself. The Church's own slowness to accept some modern scholarship and scientific methods of learning had contributed to this cleavage. Slowness to integrate faith and science—not just the physical sciences, but more especially the human sciences—created an impression that faith and science were *alternative* ways of interpreting reality. We had not understood fully enough our own axiom that 'grace builds on nature'. Pope John was looking to Catholic lay people to 'create a synthesis between science, technology and professional life on the one hand and spiritual values on the other' (PT n150).

The challenge is to do this in ways that reassure those of 'our contemporaries (who) seem to fear that a closer bond between human activity and religion might diminish the autonomy proper to human beings and to society and to the sciences' (Pastoral Constitution on the Church in the Modern World (*Gaudium et Spes*, 1965) (*GS*) 36. The Church acknowledges that it has neither a mandate nor a blue-print for social and economic planning. Its task is more radical: to reach out to the minds and hearts of those who do the social and economic planning, forming them in the vision of the gospel.

> For the Church, evangelising means bringing the good news into all the strata of humanity, and through its influence transforming humanity from within and making it new . . . (Paul VI, Apostolic Letter on Evangelisation (*Evangelii Nuntiandi*, 1975 (*EN*) 18; cf also Pope John Paul II, On 100th Anniversary of *Rerum Novarum*, *Centesimus Annus*, 1991) (*CA*) 43.

It takes a change of heart (Part I) to change the world around us (Part II).

Part I—A change of heart

It starts with each person's ongoing conversion: 'there is no new humanity if there are not first of all new persons . . . ' (Evangelisation, 18). Carl Jung acknowledged this too: 'This alone makes history, here alone do the great transformations take place. In our most private lives we are not just passive witnesses of our age, but also its makers' (quoted by D O'Leary, *The Tablet*, 22 January 2009, 12).

Personal conversion is the key to change even when the need is for institutional and structural change. Institutions and groups (whether they are business groups, trade unions, government institutions or religious institutions) develop their own customs, ethos and expectations, which considerably condition the lives of their members. This is not necessarily bad; it supports people who have the same ideals, and who feel the need for solidarity. But if for some reason change is needed, the movement for change will encounter the strong tendency of the institution to preserve the status quo, the familiar over against the unfamiliar, to say nothing of vested interests and privileges. Trying to bring about change can be likened to trying to change the direction of a moving car. Someone put the car in motion in the first place, and is regarded as being in control. But a momentum has been created that is a little larger than the powers of the people on board—and more so if they are in the back seat.

So how do we bring about change in the life of institutions and systems, given that they have a life larger than the life of their individual members?

Ultimately, it is people who drive the systems and institutions, and people who change them. The moving car does not make the decisions. Decisions are made by people. It is their change of heart that makes the difference:

> There is an approach to social issues that has been rather widely accepted and still enjoys considerable favour. It is essentially based on scientific method. A survey of the situation is made, the data collected and the most suitable remedy that the state of knowledge permits is applied. In itself, the method is unexceptionable. It is systematic and efficient. Who wants solutions based on ignorance? But as a total approach it is inadequate. It presumes that the situation and the problems are as clear and as unambiguous as rocks. It fails to recognise that what constitutes an issue, and what significance is to be attached to it, are based on one's presuppositions, values and policy. There is the tacit assumption that the problem is 'out there' to be recognised by any sane human being. On closer analysis, it appears that this approach is highly conservative. It tends to conserve the roots of the problem.
>
> The Christian approach is different and essentially radical. It invites to, in fact insists on, a fundamental shift of attention from the claimed facts 'out there' to the heart of the one who views the situation. It looks back at the one who is interpreting the facts and the situation. The person must be sure that his heart is pure, his eye clear, his love sincere, and his purposes beyond reproach. He must listen to the voice of the Lord, ready to find himself in the wrong. In listening to God's word he discovers afresh who he is in relation to God and to his brothers and sisters. This leads to a purer and fuller grasp of his responsibilities in the human and Christian communities. An awareness should gradually develop of the extent to which he himself wittingly, half-wittingly and unwittingly contributes to and connives at the situation he now regards as problematic (Rev V Hunt, unpublished paper).

Part II—To change the world

After he had said 'there is no new humanity if there are not first of all new persons', Paul VI went on to say that interior conversion contributes to the transformation of society at every level; and that conversion is incomplete if it does not do so:

> . . . Evangelisation would not be complete if it did not take account of the unceasing interplay of the gospel with our actual lives, both personal and social . . . involving an explicit message about the rights and duties of every human being, about family life . . . about life in society, about international life, peace, justice and development—and especially today, liberation (cf paragraphs 19, 29).[1]

Today we would add to that list, care for the planet. Scientists are now emphasising what indigenous religions have always believed: the well-being of the planet and human wellbeing are intimately connected. The unscrupulous despoliation of the natural environment and the ruthless oppression of people go hand in hand.[2] 'How can we separate, or even set at odds, the protection of the environment and the protection of human life . . . since the book of nature is one and indivisible?' (Pope Benedict XVI, *Annual Address to Ambassadors,* 2010).

Correcting abuse of the planet is also a matter of conversion:

> The problem is not simply economic and technological; it is it moral and spiritual. A solution at the economic level can be found only if we undergo, in the most radical way, an inner change of heart, which can lead to a change of lifestyle and sustainable patterns of consumption and production. A genuine conversion in Christ will enable us to change the way we think and act. (From Common Declaration of Pope John Paul II and Patriarch Bartholomew I of Constantinople, June 2002.) Cited on www.vatican.va).

1. This is echoed in what the Church teaches concerning the purpose of education: The method of education very frequently still in use today encourages narrow individualism. Part of the human family lives immersed in a mentality which exalts possessions. The school and the communications media are often at the service of the established order and allow only the kind of formation desired by that order; that is to say, not new persons but only copies of what people are already like.
   But education demands a renewal of heart, a renewal based on the recognition of sin both in individuals and in society. It will also inculcate a truly and entirely human way of life, including justice, love and simplicity. It will likewise awaken a critical sense, which will lead us to reflect on the society in which we live and on its values; it will make people ready to renounce those values when they cease to promote justice for everyone (*Justice in the World*, Bishops' Synod, 1971, paragraphs 50, 51).
2. This happens not only where indigenous peoples are driven from their ancestral lands to urban slums, but also where economic policies allow lop-sided loyalty to shareholders and top executives, without equal regard for what happens to those who contribute to the economy by their labour and sacrifices.

For some years, Catholic social teaching has taught that the economic order is only one aspect of authentic human development. It finds its own proper perspectives and correctives within holistic human development, which includes the human capacity for transcendence and the need for freedom, social responsibility, responsible stewardship for the planet, and the economic development of others. This is why social and economic planning are not ethically neutral: they are part of the wider agenda of making human life more genuinely human. That objective must be built into the processes. This differs from giving free reign to market forces and redressing the imbalances afterwards.

In his Encyclical *On Integral Human Development, Caritas in Veritate*, 2009, chapter 3 (*CV*), Pope Benedict goes further: economies are not sufficiently human if based only on the 'logic of exchange'—this in exchange for that. The practice of gratuitousness, compassion, giving and forgiving needs to be built into social and economic life. This is because human beings, by nature, are beings whose existence has been freely given to them; it was not owed. And so we are never more true to our own nature than when giving and forgiving, and never more like the One in whose image we are made.

It is no longer possible to pursue 'justice', even within national economies and in international trade, without factoring in the needs of the world's poor. They must be included *as of right*—not as the recipients of 'charity', but as participants in the economies of a world that belongs to all.

The Church needs to be seen as an unwavering defender of the *human*, and the gospel as making human life more human.[3] Historically, the Church has not always done this well. Sometimes it has been slow to recognise values that were inherent in the dignity of personhood, and sometimes it has opposed them.

Nevertheless, faithful to Judeo Christian Revelation, it holds high its belief that openness to God (whether explicit or implicit) is essential to what makes us truly human. This gives the Church, despite its own failures, insight into the very values that Modernity itself esteems, namely the

3. Cf GS 38; John Paul II, *The Redeemer of Human Race* (*Redemptor Hominis*, 1981) (*RH*) 13.

yearning for tolerance, self-expression, dialogue, human rights, participation, democracy, pluralism and solidarity. These are all about life-in-relationship-with-others. The Church is better positioned to promote these values than is any ideology that looks no further than the individual's understanding what it means to be human. Post-Modernity has it that the individual's claims are self-validating. Not surprisingly, therefore, people's perceptions of freedom, authenticity, honesty, love, tolerance, equality and human rights are all being skewed by the expectation that they ultimately mean whatever the individual believes they mean.

As Cardinal Murphy-O'Connor has said of modern secularism, those who have an 'impoverished understanding of what it means to be human . . . in the end have no satisfactory defence against the instrumentalisation of the person' (*The Tablet*, 7 March 2009).

The Church has something more radical to offer humanity because its gospel is about a love for life and for the world that does not stop at what can be merited, earned, deserved or found useful. Nothing more fully embraces the world *as it really is* than love poured out where it is *not* merited. That really is love for the world! And that is precisely what the gospel teaches about God's love for the world, and what our love needs to be like: 'love one another as I have loved you' (Jn 13:34).

To be a credible witness to God's love for the world, the Church needs to overcome what Daniel O'Leary has called 'a deadly and deep-seated dualism dividing the holy from the human'. He says that 'even though this dichotomy was definitively ended the night that God became human, the body of the Church is still infected with this debilitating virus' (*The Tablet*, 18 April 2009, 10).

This ancient dualism presupposes that loving God and loving the world are in some way opposed to each other. We need to be convinced that—as Karl Rahner put it: 'love for God and love for the world are in *direct*, not inverse, proportion'. To talk of 'balancing' the two is no help because the very idea of balancing presupposes that more of one means less of the other, that is *inverse* proportion. What is needed is their proper *integration*, which comes about when our love for God and love for God's creation lead into and enhance each other (direct proportion). Pope Paul VI once said that we must love and look after the world as we do our own flesh. And for the same reasons, we need to rejoice in the findings of science. They extol the glory of God.

This letter has been about the gospel 'transforming humanity' starting with personal conversion and reaching out into every sphere of social, political and economic life. This is above all the apostolate of lay men and women. It is the way they exercise their priestly-prophetic ministry based on their baptism/confirmation. It is the 'work of human hands' and minds that they bring into the celebration of Eucharist. It is worship.

St Irenaeus taught that 'the glory of God is the human being fully alive . . . ' It is God we honour by promoting the dignity and the destiny of every person.

This is what Pope John Paul II echoed when he said 'man (sic) is the primary route the Church must travel in fulfilling its mission—the way traced by Christ himself'. (*RH* 14)

A renewed Church takes that route. It affirms the goodness of all that God has made, the sacredness of human life, the dignity of every person, the need to call 'wrong' whatever violates them, and God's redeeming love making all things new.[4]

This newness is ultimately a newness that is beyond our ability to bring about, and comes to us from God. It is pure gift, and it is undeserved mercy:

> Then I saw a new heaven and a new earth . . . I saw the holy city, the new Jerusalem coming down out of heaven from God . . .
>
> (God) will wipe away every tear from their eyes. Death will be no more; mourning and crying and pain will be no more, for the first things have passed away . . .
>
> And the One who was seated on the throne said, 'See I am making all things new.' (cf Rev 21:1–5, NRSV Catholic Bible Press, 1993).

4. The leadership of recent popes in the development of Catholic social teaching helps to account for the high regard in which they are held by many who do not share our faith.

In the meantime, everything we do to promote human dignity and human rights matters, because love and justice, compassion and forgiveness, beauty and joy are the signs of something greater than sin, suffering and death—signs that the new heaven and new earth are already breaking in on us; that Christ is risen and shares his risen life with us. They are the language of hope. A renewed Church will speak that language more loudly.

The Church is a credible sign of the future it speaks about 'in the measure that it proves effective for the reign of love and of justice here on earth' (Juan Alfaro SJ, *Theology of Justice in the World*, Commission Justice and Peace, Vatican City 1973, 44).

Letter Three

Seeing God

Tena koe e Rangimarie,

I was deeply impressed by the goodness, faith and *joie de vivre* of your class of school leavers. Afterwards, you told me of your visit to the Cistercian monastery at Kopua and asked me whether there was anything like that 'for girls'. I came away wondering how many young people are let down by us because we underestimate them! You had intuited that a full life involves God.

When St Irenaeus said 'the glory of God is the human being fully alive', he added—in the same sentence—'and what makes us fully alive is seeing God'. Being fully alive is a way of being that comes from a way of seeing, and loving.

There is a way of seeing reality as it really is. This means seeing it as that which might never have existed, but does. Its very existence results from a choice God did not have to make, but did. Just facing its existence, simply letting ourselves be present to it, can lead to the experience of deep wonder and amazement. We are seeing what Pope John Paul II called 'the extraordinary side of the ordinary'.[1]

What is true of everything around us is true also of our self. We do not begin to know ourselves, let alone God, until we know that our own

---

1. This is necessarily a personal experience, but we can let ourselves be led to it: 'because artists and writers and musicians have looked at what is before their eyes with absorbed attention in order to learn to love them, we can, by watching where they plant their steps, do the same. They invite us to join in the dance of words and paint and music'. Michael Main, *Learning to Dance* (London: DLT, 2001), 137.

existence had its origins in a choice God did not have to make but did. It was, and is, a pure gift. The mystery and the wonder of this opens our eyes to how greatly we have been loved.

This discovery empowers us to love in return; to move beyond just fulfilling a duty, to being *in love*, with God and all that God has made. Being in love is always a different way of being—and seeing. The world looks different. But it hasn't changed; we ourselves have become more truly human, more alive. This is the calling of every human being, each made in the image of God, who is love.

This way of being transforms religious practice from mere routine and duty into desire and delight, which is surely at the heart of renewal. It is transforming. And it is what Pope John Paul meant when, echoing the Council, he told the New Zealand bishops during their 1998 *Ad Limina* visit 'to make a systematic effort in your dioceses and parishes to open new doors to the experience of Christian prayer and contemplation . . . '

Karl Rahner memorably said 'the Christian of tomorrow will be a mystic, one who has experienced something, or he/she will be nothing.'[2] Teachers attest that this 'experience of something' can be appreciated even by young children when given times for prayerful stillness and silence. In this way they develop the *capacity* for contemplation.

They miss much who never developed the capacity for stillness, silence and contemplation. Dominican Timothy Radcliffe tells of his experience watching the film *Into Great Silence* featuring the mother house of the Carthusian monks:

> It lasts three hours and almost nothing is said. Alas, when I watched it in St Louis it should have been called *Into the Great Popcorn Crunching*. The reactions of the audience were fascinating. There were two groups, the retired and students, the only people free on a weekday afternoon. The retired were unenthusiastic and some left before the film finished. I overheard remarks such as 'Why pay to

---

2. *Theological Investigations*, Volume XIX, 115; Volume XX, 149. A decade earlier, Raimon Panikkar had said: 'In this crucible of the modern world only the mystic will survive.' *The Cosmotheandric Experience, Emerging Religious Consciousness*, edited by Scott Eastham (Mryknoll: Orbis 1993), 122.

> watch paint drying?' . . . But the young could not bring themselves to leave. They watched until the last credit was over. They savoured the silence, as if they had waited for it for a long time. (*Why Go to Church?* [London: Continuum, 2008], 30–31).

But most are missing out on the experience of stillness and silence. This is why their life-choices often lack the depth that comes from experiencing God's presence in their lives. There are life-choices that only come on to our horizons when we experience the mystery of our own existence and the need for meaning.

Opportunities for reflective awareness are diminishing as life is driven more and more by greed, that is, economic policies that intrude on the time and space that others need for a truly human life, and the desperation of those who drive themselves into fragmented living and increasing insecurity. If being 'fully alive' and 'seeing God' go together, so do *not* seeing God and *not* being fully alive.

'Seeing' God in this contemplative way is knowing the God in whom 'we live and move and have our being' (Acts 17:8). St Augustine reminded us that God is 'closer to us than we are to ourselves'.[3] We don't look for God 'out there'. We are *in* God. This is what the contemplative tradition has known all the time. The author of the *Cloud of Unknowing* says 'God is your being, and what you are, you are in God' (which does not mean that

3. Some make much of the fact that people can no longer think of God 'up there', 'out there'. But the problem is not our changed understanding of the universe. It is ideology: both the ideological fundamentalism of those (for example, evangelical 'creationists') who fight to retain interpretations of scripture that science has discredited, and the ideological reductionism of those who deny the existence of everything that cannot be known by science (for example, Richard Dawkins).

   After paying tribute to the tradition of the Enlightenment which 'has given us modern science and much freedom', Timothy Radcliffe OP reminds us that if knowing is reduced to the dimensions of detached scientific observation, we end up doubting everything that cannot be known in that way. 'Looking down a microscope is a useful way of looking at the world, but if we try to look at each other only through microscopes, we will not see each other's goodness which is the deepest truth of our being.' *Crisis of Truth in our Society*, 15 November 2004, www.*domlife.org/dlc/Resources/CrisisInTruthRadcliffe.*

   Renewal looks beyond the Church itself to the Church's credibility and mission, and so it requires that Catholics be able to show how faith and reason support each other. Yet, how central is Pope John Paul II's great Encyclical *On Faith and Reason* in our programmes of religious education and adult education?

we *are* God). Between God and the soul there is no in between (Julian of Norwich); God is in creation as the voice is in the song (A de Mello SJ).

Conversion is the grace and process of overcoming the *illusion* of having an existence separate from God. 'Union (with God) is seen to be the fundamental reality, and separateness the highly filtered mental perception.' (Martin Laird, *Into the Silent Land* [Oxford: Oxford University Press, 2006], 10).

'We all exist solely for this—to be the human place God has chosen for his presence, his manifestation, his epiphany' (Thomas Merton, quoted by D O'Leary, *The Tablet*, 16 May 2009, 16). God's presence comes to visibility in your life, your love, your creativity, your joy, your compassion, your prayer—what our tradition calls sacramentality.

Union with God in this way is not just about 'God and me'. It is union with God who is 'over all, through all, and in all' (Eph 4:6). Our love becomes as God's love, which is *for all*. It is a *communion* of love.

Letter Four

Communion

Dear Naomi,

Your letter reminded me of TS Eliot's lines:

> We shall not cease from exploration
> and the end of all our exploring
> will be to arrive where we started
> and know the place for the first time. (*Little Gidding*)

In your explorations you discovered God's presence outside the household of your ancestral faith. Then, in re-discovering your own faith you found it already contained all that you went looking for—especially in its mystical tradition. After all, the life, death and resurrection of Jesus give historical visibility and focus to what God's Holy Spirit is doing throughout the world. Cf Decree on the Church's Missionary Activity (*Ad Gentes*, 1965), (*AG*) 4.

Communion—with Christ

Union with God comes about through our union with Christ. 'You belong to Christ, and Christ belongs to God.' (1 Cor 3:23).[1] This is not something we have to achieve; it was so from the beginning; all we can do is be amazed, and say thank you.

> He is the image of the unseen God . . .
> . . . in him were created all things in heaven and on earth…

1. See also Ephesians, *passim*; 1 Corinthians 15:20–23; Romans 8:19–20.

> . . . before anything was created, he existed,
> and he holds all things in unity . . . (cf Col 1:15–20)

Nevertheless, this union with God is a *personal relationship* with God. It takes flesh in our relationship with Christ. The Holy Spirit draws us into Christ's risen life and his relationship with the Father. This relationship with Christ and with all who are united to him—this communion—*is the Church* at the deepest level of its being.[2]

If being the Church is rooted in our relationship with Christ, then renewal of the Church comes through *deepening our relationship* with Him. This is why every one of us can contribute to the Church's renewal. And why the saints do most of all.

Deepening our relationship with Christ involves knowing him more intimately. It helps to look into the gospels to see how much he meant to the people who got close to him in those days. *What He meant to them reveals him to us.*

In his presence they experienced deep reassurance. Just listening to him, they *knew* they mattered to God. In discovering how much they meant to God, they discovered *themselves.*

Now that he is risen, he is as truly present to us as he was to them. We can speak to him about what happened during his life and what is happening in ours. Spending time in his company we discover what they discovered. We too were included when he said of his disciples 'I have called you friends'. In the deepening of this friendship, faith, hope and love come to life in us. Have you sometimes lain awake at night, perhaps anxious about something the new day will bring, and remembered that He had nights like that too? And have you used these times to speak to Him intimately about how it was for Him, and how your life and His are connected?

Another name for all this intimacy and spending time with him is prayer. Allowing ourselves to be *drawn into his prayer* we are being formed in his ways of thinking and loving and being for others. This affects how

---

2. According to the 1985 Extraordinary Synod of Bishops, understanding the Church as this 'communion' was 'the central and fundamental idea of the Council's documents'. (*Origins*, 19 December 1985, 448)

we think about everything else. This 'turn-around' in our thinking and priorities is our deepening *conversion*—and renewal. Our conversion is *to Him*; all else follows from this.

The effectiveness of the Church's work depends on this deeper relationship with Christ. As Pope John Paul II put it in his Apostolic letter On the Great Jubilee of the Year 2000 (*Novo Millennio Ineunte* 2001 (*NMI*) pastoral planning must be 'profoundly rooted in contemplation and prayer' (15); and 'set in relationship to holiness' (30); that it presupposes 'education in prayer' (34) and a 'spirituality of communion' (43).

Communion—with one another

Communion with Christ brings us into communion with one another. It is not an individualistic 'spirituality'. Jesus himself seemed to expect that in accepting his friendship we are also accepting his friends—all of them. Our relationship with him is personal, but hardly private.

The privatisation of faith began with the claim that 'man-made' religion got in the way of simple direct faith in Christ based on the scriptures. However, this over-simplified separation of 'religion' and 'faith' has led to an even wider gap: the scriptures themselves, and Christ, and the very idea of historic revelation, are now lumped in with 'religion' and dispensed with in favour of 'spirituality'.

This is a trajectory that becomes progressively more subjective and humanly demeaning. David Ranson puts it this way:

> Without intellectual accountability, 'spirituality' is adrift and free to meander into 'spiritualism': the sense of an extra-terrestrial world inhabited by celestial and spirit beings of one kind or another with whom immediate and direct contact is both sought and acquired. Mostly, this has the objective of the manipulation of forces of power that give answer to life's powerlessness and apparent chaos. Such, however, is a sophisticated form of escapism . . . (*Across the Great Divide*, (St Paul's, NSW, Australia, 2002), 16)

That kind of 'spirituality' is the off-spring of ideological individualism, which can only self-destruct.

There is no point in trying to be an island—even a spiritual one. It is the faith *of the community* rooted in *historic events* and *historic revelation*, that is needed to properly interpret and validate the individual's 'religious experience'. Religious experience draws on the experience of love and belonging, goodness and beauty, and of the mystery of evil. The community that commemorates the life, teaching, suffering, dying and rising of Christ is uniquely placed to interpret those experiences.

The community that is able to interpret religious experience is, in its turn, constantly enriched and enlivened by receiving into its own life the individual's religious experiences. The individual and the community are renewed together.

Letter Five

For Mission and Through Mission

Dear Bishops gathering for the Extraordinary Synod on Renewal,

As you know, sharing in God's work of 'making all things new' is how the Church transcends itself in carrying out its mission. In and through carrying out its mission, *the Church itself* is made new.

There was not first a Church to which was given a mission. First were missions—the 'sending' of the Son and the 'sending' of the Holy Spirit. Through them creation is being drawn into the communion which is God's life.

To 'unite all things in Christ' was the plan God had in mind 'before the world was made'. This was the 'mystery of God's purpose' which had been 'kept secret for endless ages', and that God would 'act upon when the times had run their course'. It was for this that the Son and Holy Spirit were sent (see especially Ephesians chapters 1 & 3; Colossians, chapter 1, Romans 8:18–24; Revelation 21:1–5.). Through our union with Christ in the power of the Holy Spirit that original plan continues to unfold. The Church comes into existence out of what the Son and the Holy Spirit are *still doing*.

If that is where the Church comes from and what it exists for, then that is also where renewal comes from, and what renewal is for. Renewal has a goal beyond the Church itself, that is, to serve the mission of the Son and Holy Spirit.

Renewal requires a bigness of mind and heart worthy of the bigness of God's plan. It is striking how often the words 'bold', 'boldly' and 'boldness' recur in the New Testament scriptures. It is pusillanimity and fear of making mistakes that cripple. It is a mistake to confuse 'prudence' with a kind of tutiorism—resorting always to the way that seems safest. In the work of the gospel, prudence itself can require boldness.

Pope John XXIII was right: the Church on the eve of Vatican II stood in need of a 'new Pentecost'. That is what transformed timid men into great apostles (cf Acts 2:4). When he announced the Council, it was for the purpose of 'renewal'. We who are responsible for implementing the Council today do well to re-read what he said, and find ourselves refreshed by the humility, courage and joy that inspired people then, and can still do so today.

The courage called for is that which is big enough to let the Church's mission shape its identity:

> . . . (The) Church will suffer the loss of its shape as it undergoes a death, and all the more so, the more purely it lives from its source and is consequently less concerned with preserving its shape. In fact, it will not concern itself with affirming its shape but with promoting the world's salvation; as for the shape in which God will raise it from its death to serve the world, it will entrust (that) to the Holy Spirit. (Hans Urs von Balthasar, The Three Forms of Hope, quoted in Weigel's *Soul of the World* William B Eerdmans Publishing Co. Grand Rapids, Michegan, 1996, 41.

This means that the Church finds it identity not in juxtaposition to its mission, or prior to it, but in and through carrying out its mission.

Faithfulness to its mission is also how the Church best secures its 'continuity'—because its mission is always the same. Continuities related to ecclesiastical traditions are never more important that the continuity of faithfulness to the Church's mission. At their best they serve and express that mission.

Catholic identity is a 'live' issue today. Kasper was thinking historically when he observed that 'if the Church worries about its identity it risks a loss of relevance; if on the other hand it struggles for relevance it may forfeit its identity' (Walter Kasper, *Jesus the Christ*, [B & O London/Paulist NY, 1997 [London, 1997], 15). We need to see that the issue of continuity and the issue of identity are resolved in the same way, that is, through radical faithfulness to the Church's mission.

It is tempting to want to protect the Church—like the man in Jesus' parable who hid the gold coin entrusted to him. He was condemned for not risking it on the market. The Council was being faithful to the gospel when it consciously chose to go beyond its reflections on the Church to reflect on the Church ministering in a broken and hurting world:

> The joys and the hopes, the griefs and the anxieties of the people of this age, especially those who are poor or in any way afflicted, these too are the joys and hopes, the griefs and anxieties of the followers of Christ. Nothing that is genuinely human fails to find an echo in their hearts (Pastoral Constitution on the Church in the Modern World (*Gaudium et Spes*), 1963 (*GS*) 1).

To be true to its mission, and therefore to itself, the Church must be the bearer of hope to those most in need of it. And so in your deliberations at this Synod, you could hardly do better than remember a brother bishop who has already modeled the ecclesiology you are looking for. In doing for his people what *they* most needed, he did for the Church what *it* most needed. The gospel would have it that the institution that strives to save itself will lose itself; but if it loses itself in loving service, it will save itself.

> The Church will only be a bearer of credible hope to humanity if it stands with the poor, with all who are victims of sin, injustice and violence. If we walk with them, as Archbishop Oscar Romero did, we will embody the good news that the world so longs for (D Brackley SJ, reported by *National Catholic Reporter*, 25 March 2010).

Letter Six

Inculturation

Dear Bishops at the Extraordinary Synod on Renewal,

Your discussions on renewal have moved naturally into discussions on inculturation. The bigness of mind and heart that I spoke of in my earlier letter are required especially for the work of inculturation.

Taking differences of time and culture into account is necessary for effective evangelisation:

> (The Church's programme) does not change with the shifts of time and cultures . . . though it takes account of time and culture *for the sake of true dialogue and effective communication* (John Paul II, Apostolic Letter at the Close of the Great Jubilee of the Year 2000 (*Novo Millennio Ineunte*, 2001) 29; (emphasis added).

To reach people and transform their lives, the gospel must reach and transform their cultures:

> What matters is to evangelise man's culture and cultures, not in a purely decorative way as it were by applying a thin veneer, but in a vital way, in depth and right to the very roots . . . (Pope Paul VI, Apostolic Letter on Evangelisation, *Evangelii Nuntiandi,* 1975 (*EN*) 20, 62.

In this way, the gospel itself is being transposed into different ways of learning, teaching and expressing the faith. Inculturation involves a

> transposition of the Gospel . . . in the field of liturgical expression, and in the areas of catechesis, theological formulation, secondary ecclesial structures and ministries (*Ibid*, 63).

The resulting pluriformity reflects the catholicity and the history of the Catholic Church. Insistence on maximum uniformity is not more Catholic; it is *less* Catholic, and less expressive of Catholicity.

Moreover, we should expect tensions, misunderstandings, and even some mistakes, as the Church moves—on all of these fronts—towards being more truly world-wide.

Clearly, inculturation involves 'the areas of catechesis, theological formulation, secondary ecclesial structures and ministries', and not just 'liturgical expression'. But the official Church seems to experience some ambivalence even about allowing genuine inculturation in the music of the liturgy:

> . . . while respecting various styles and different and highly praiseworthy traditions, I desire, in accordance with the request advanced by the Synod Fathers, that Gregorian chant be suitably esteemed and employed as the chant proper to the Roman liturgy. (Pope Benedict XVI, On Integral Human Development in Charity and Truth, (*Sacramentum Caritatis*, 2009) (*SC*) 42.[1]

In 1994 the Congregation for Divine Worship and Sacraments issued an Instruction applying articles 37–40 of *The Constitution on the Liturgy* dealing with inculturation. The Instruction uses Pope John Paul II's definition of inculturation as

> the incarnation of the Gospel in autonomous cultures and at the same time the introduction of those cultures into the life of the Church. (Letter on the Apostles to the Slavic Peoples, 1985, 21; also

1. In view of how greatly the music of Africa, Asia and the countries of Melanesia and Polynesia (to name only some) all differ from Gregorian chant, it seems inevitable that there will need to be further variations of the Roman Missal (as was done for the dioceses of Zaire) in order to respect those differences. See the 1994 Instruction *Varietates Legitimae*, paragraph 40.

the Encyclical On the Permanent Validity of the Church's Missionary Mandate (*Redemptoris Missio*, 1990), (*RM*) 52.

The term 'incarnation' clearly intends a deeper integration of faith and culture than the term 'adaptation' suggests. In fact, the Instruction itself acknowledges that the word 'adaptation' suggests 'modifications of a somewhat transitory and external nature' (paragraph 4). Yet it spite of this, the Cardinal Prefect's accompanying letter to the Bishops' Conferences (March 1994) is, to say the least, tentative when it speaks of the need to 'incorporate opportune adaptations'. Even the Encyclical *Redemptoris Missio*, in spite of its stated preference for the term 'inculturation' lapses frequently into using the term 'adaptation'.[2]

I suspect that inculturation will be only superficial until it reaches the depth implied by Karl Rahner in his memorable words:

> . . . theologically speaking, there are three great epochs in Church history, of which the third has only just begun. First, the short period of Jewish Christianity. Second, the period of the Church in a distinct cultural region, namely that of Hellenism and of European culture and civilisation. Third, the period in which the sphere of the Church's life is in fact the entire world. These three periods signify three essential and different basic situations for Christianity and its preaching . . .
>
> . . . the coming-to-be of a world Church . . . does not mean just a quantitative increase in the previous Church, but rather contains a theological break in Church history that still lacks conceptual clarity, and can scarcely be compared with anything except the transition from Jewish to Gentile Christianity. ('Towards a Fundamental Theological Interpretation of Vatican II', *Theological Studies*, December 1979: 721, 726, 727).

2. Of course, the Christian faith is already inculturated by reason of its origins in historical events, and these cannot be shed as it were in favour of a fresh start in each different culture. For reasons like this, Cardinal Ratzinger preferred the term 'interculturality', meaning a process of 'reciprocal refinement and combination' (Address to Asian Bishops' Conferences, 1993). I think the point is rather academic because not all historical developments are constitutive of the Christian faith, and the kind of 'transpositions' Pope Paul VI spoke of do not imply any detachment from its historical origins.

It was not easy for the early Church to break out of its Jewish matrix to become incarnate in the cultures of Rome and Greece, which later formed the basis of European culture. It will be no less painful for the Church of our day to reach beyond the confines of predominantly European thought-patterns to become incarnate in every culture of the world. But failure to inculturate is failure to evangelise.

The Catholic Church in Aotearoa New Zealand has not evangelised at the depth or the breadth described above in the words of Pope Paul VI. Instead of 'transposing' the gospel, we have merely adapted European ways of teaching, serving and expressing the faith. We are all the losers by this, for reasons that are implicit in Pope John Paul II's words at Auckland, New Zealand, in 1986:

> The strengths of Maori culture are often the very values which modern society is in danger of losing: an acknowledgement of the spiritual dimension of every aspect of life; a profound reverence for nature and the environment; a sense of community assuring every individual that he or she belongs; loyalty to family and a great willingness to share; an acceptance of death as part of life and a capacity to grieve and mourn the dead in a human way.
>
> As you rightly treasure your culture, let the gospel of Christ continue to penetrate and permeate it, confirming your sense of identity as a unique part of God's household.
>
> It is as Maori that the Lord calls you; it is as Maori that you belong to the Church, the one body of Christ.

The first Catholic missionaries (who came from France from 1838 on) initially identified with the Maori people, and the early European immigrants took their place within patterns of Church life centred around the needs and customs of the Maori people. But when the missionaries turned their attention more to the needs of the increasing immigrant population, a more European model of Church life developed. Thereafter, Maori Catholics were provided for through a 'Maori mission' that eventually ran parallel with parish life. The Maori mission provided a very person-centred ministry to Maori and respected their right to learn and practise the Catholic faith in ways that were culturally natural to them.[3]

But the parallelism of parish life and Maori mission resulted in parishes becoming mono-cultural in a non-Maori sense. The bishops had entrusted the Maori mission to religious orders, and neglected to train diocesan priests for ministry to Maori. Now it is very difficult even for practising Catholic Maori to feel genuinely 'at home' in most of our Sunday congregations and parish activities.

Moreover, faced with the incursions of colonisation, and experiencing a deep sense of loss, many Maori have felt down the years, and still feel, a need to cling to certain pre-Christian beliefs as a way of retaining their own identity. Various amalgams of Christian faith and pre-Christian religion, even among Catholic Maori, have resulted from this (see *Prophetic Histories: The People of the Maramatanga,* Karen Sinclair, Bridget Williams Books, Wellington, New Zealand, 2002).

Those who are over-cautious about inculturation should be more concerned about syncretistic amalgams of Christian faith and pre-Christian religion that can develop where inculturation has been neglected or inadequate. Perhaps they have not yet heard Catholics pray to other gods, nor wondered why.[4]

3. Tribute should also be made to the heroic and successful work done by other Christian missionaries for nearly half a century before the Catholic missionaries arrived.
4. The inter-penetration of the spiritual and material in the Maori world-view allows the 'atua' (gods) to be understood variously, as (i) personifications of different parts of creation and its eco systems (cf St Francis of Assisi's prayers); (ii) created spiritual powers; (iii) kaitiaki (guardians) (cf Hebrew and Christian 'angels'). In any event, these atua belong to creation, and are not gods in the sense that the ancient Romans and Greeks had their gods. Maori religion acknowledged one Supreme Being, Io. The atua reflected the divine presence in the world (cf Pan*en*theism). This understanding of the atua enabled the old people to welcome Christianity as an elevation, not a violation, of their own beliefs. However, a real problem arises because some younger Maori do not properly understand older Maori belief, and they pray to the atua in the same way that Christians pray to God. In this way, what were previously just personifications of God's presence in nature become personal gods; (instead of Pan*en*theism, Pantheism.) Proper inculturation would enable them to identity more completely with our Christian and Catholic faith.

Some of the difficulties and fears inhibiting inculturation derive from the Church's excessive euro-centrism. It is no disrespect to any recent pope to point out that we are all limited by our cultural horizons, no matter how well informed. For all the wisdom, insight and spiritual leadership the Church has received from its popes down the years, and not least of all in recent years, it will nevertheless be a landmark moment in the move to more genuine inculturation when the Church is given a non-European, non-Europeanised pope. There is more to this than symbolism. If culture can be called the most overlooked educational influence in most lives (Michael Warren), it can also be called the most overlooked horizon bearing upon every person's perceptions of reality.

Letter Seven

'Receiving' the Council

Dear 'unsure parishioner',

Thank you for your letter. Because the New Zealand headquarters of the Society of St Pius X is located within your parish, it is not surprising that you often hear their claim that they are the stronger for not accepting the Second Vatican Council, and their scepticism about how the Council was supposed to renew the Church.

The Second Vatican Council was beyond doubt a special moment in God's providence for the Church when it needed to better equip itself for evangelising in a very different world. The world it was used to was changing fast. Subsequent over-interpretations of the Council and excesses by some, and attempts by others to back away from the Council, are both due very largely to *inadequate catechesis*. Some of the confusion that became manifest after the Council actually had its origins in the inadequacies of pre-conciliar catechetical formation. Before the Council there was almost no catechesis to prepare people for what was to come, and following the Council opportunities for adult education in the faith were not taken up by many Catholics (and, sadly, in some countries not even offered). Sound adult education in the faith is able to show very clearly the Council's continuity with the Catholic tradition, and is able to obviate much of today's anxiety about Catholic identity.

The authors of the five volume history of the Second Vatican Council edited by Giuseppe Alberigo and Joseph Komonchak (Leuven/Maryknoll, Peeters/Orbis, 1995, ff) give us deep insights into what normally happens after a general Council of the Church—in the case of those Councils that have made a significant impact. The Second Vatican Council fits the pattern. I add my comments to their insights.

First, the Council itself is an event that releases new enthusiasm and expectations. Writing at the end of the Council, Joseph Ratzinger who was present at the Council as a theological adviser, describes the experience of the Council as a 'spiritual awakening'. Comparing the sessions of the Council he says that

> the Episcopate became more open-minded from year to year. From somewhat timid and tentative beginnings, in which a few spokesmen had to carry a whole host of astonished listeners with them, discussion advanced to the point where in 1964 it became extremely frank and did not evade issues any longer . . . This spiritual awakening . . . was the great and irrevocable event of the Council. It was more important than the texts it passed, for these texts could only voice a part of the new life that had been awakened. (*Theological Highlights of Vatican II* [Paulist Press, Deus Books, NY, 1966], 138).

In the immediate aftermath some simplistic interpretations of the Council emerged, sometimes as a kind of critical reaction to the style of the pre-Council period. This has been followed by a period of unsettlement, difficulties and turmoil. It could hardly be otherwise because new ways involve some letting go of previous ways. Social anthropologists assure us that 'chaos' is a normal prelude to renewal. (Chaos just as surely results from failure to take up the Council's call for renewal, and eventually forces the issue of renewal.)

But there can also be loss. Raymond E Brown has shown (when discussing divisions within the early Johanine communities and at the Reformation) how polemic can lead to divisions that are wider than the issues originally in dispute, and to a 'loss of heritage' on both sides. He sees a less dramatic example of this in the way that polemics after the Second Vatican Council illustrated the claim that 'often what is passed on to the next generation is only what was fought over'.

> The new developments that had affected the lives of the teachers were the substance of the message communicated to the children, but concomitantly this involved a neglect of much Catholic tradition that was *not* affected by the Council—the distinctive presuppositions of Catholic life. As a result the generation that grew up in the 1970s, while being very aware of some new outlooks of Vatican II, were often painfully ignorant of much of their Catholic heritage.

> Those who taught the new were at times deaf to cries about the loss of the old, equating all such cries with a traditionalist rejection of the Council. (*The Churches The Apostles Left Behind*, [Paulist Press, NY 1984], 117–118.)

What is required of leaders during this time is deep personal commitment to the vision of the Council. It is not the time for panic or retreat to positions and attitudes that the Council intended to supersede. It is one thing to correct misinterpretations of the Council. It is not helpful, on the other hand, to speak of 'reforming the reform' because that suggests that the Council itself needs to be corrected. Nor is it the time to opt out.

Moving beyond the unsettled phase involves something deeper than logic. The transition can be enhanced by deeper trust in one another, and by re-telling the stories of our common origins. The Gospels and Acts of the Apostles have the power that story-telling has, and the power of God's word speaking to us now.

The third and most important phase takes the Church beyond merely institutional changes. It is the 'reception' of the Council by the whole Church. This involves the consciousness of all the faithful and their sense of what really is the Church's faith. Under the formative influence of the Holy Spirit the ancient tradition *is re-received in new expressions.* In this way, all the faithful participate in the work of the Council. Its work takes flesh and blood in them.

The whole Church is nourished by those springs of renewal that fed into the Council, namely a renewed and deeper appreciation of the scriptures, the liturgy, the experience of ecumenism, and of engagement with the contemporary world. In this way, the whole previous teaching of the Church is 're-discovered' (Pope John Paul II's word) in the light of the Council. As he said: the 'new' grows out of the 'old' and the 'old' finds fuller expression in the 'new'. Apostolic Letter On Preparation for the Jubilee Year (*Tertio Millennio Adveniente*, 1994 (*TMA*) 18.

The process of 'receiving' takes time; there are no short-cuts via authoritative decrees.

The journey from where the Church was (but isn't now) to where it needs to be (but isn't yet) can be an unsettling time. Some are tempted to go back. But going back to what used to be there is like finding oneself in a hall of mirrors. It also has its own hazards.[1] The problem often comes from a misunderstanding of 'traditions'. Joseph Ratzinger describes a conflict of mentalities at the Council, that well describes a problem we still face today:

> On the one hand there is a mentality which is purely formal in approach and takes the current legal status of the Church as the only standard for its considerations. It therefore regards any change beyond these limits as an extremely dangerous step. The conservatism of this view is based on its aloofness from history and so it basically suffers from a lack of Tradition—ie of openness to the totality of Christian history. It is important that we see this because it gives us an insight into the inner pattern of the opposing alignments of thought in the Council, often mistakenly described as an opposition between progressives and conservatives. It would be more correct to speak of a contrast between historical thinking and formally juridical thinking. The 'progressives' (at least the large majority of them) were in fact concerned precisely with 'tradition', with a new awareness of both the breadth and depth of what had been handed down in Christian Tradition. This was where they found the norms for renewal which permitted them to be fearless and broad in their outlook. It was an outlook which came from the intrinsic catholicity of the Church (*Theological Highlights* . . . 114–115).

Joseph Ratzinger (quoted earlier) had spoken of the 'spiritual awakening (that) was the great and irrevocable event of the Council—more important than the texts it passed . . . ' The ongoing renewal of the Church taps into that re-awakening which undergirds the texts. Addressing the Extraordinary Synod of Bishops in 1985, Cardinal Krol reminded the assembly that

1. A former member of, and seminary professor for, the Priestly Fraternity of St Peter speaks of that group's 'ideological fixation on the 1962 rubrics'. A former member of Regnum Christi (the lay affiliates of the Legionnaires of Christ) speaks of the Legionaries' dependency on their founder's rules and example down to 'even his style of hair and glasses' (*The Tablet*, 11 February 2009). The Archbishop of Baltimore reports that those who leave the group suffer from 'deep psychological distress for dependency and need prolonged counselling akin to deprogramming' (*The Tablet*, 7 March 2009). Those Catholics who still hanker for some of our earlier methods of formation and regimentation need to reflect on why the Church needed to move away from them—and not turn back.

> The Pope did not call us to celebrate a mini-Council or to change or correct Vatican II, but to re-live that extraordinary experience of ecclesial communion which was one of the distinctive notes of Vatican II, to offer us an occasion together to exchange experiences about the way in which we have translated the decrees of Vatican II into the life of the Church, and to deepen the application of the Council to the needs of the Church and of the world of our time (*Origins*, 19 December 1985, 427).

In its Final Report, the Synod called for

> a deeper reception of the Council. And this requires four successive phases: a deeper and more extensive knowledge of the Council, its interior assimilation, its loving affirmation, and its implementation . . . (*Origins*, 19 December 1985, 445).

We all contribute to the renewal of the Church by re-receiving our Catholic tradition in the ways the Council re-presents it.

Letter Eight

Pastoral

Dear bishop,

This will be your first experience of a General Synod of Bishops in Rome. You will learn much from the other bishops precisely because they reflect the faith as it is lived in their local churches. Your contribution to the universal Church will depend on you trusting your experience of the faith of the people you serve in your diocese and country.

During discussions at the Second Vatican Council on the nature of the Church, the need was felt to look not only at the Church itself, but also at its relationship with the world around it. Looking inwards at the Church itself produced the Dogmatic Constitution on the Church (*Lumen Gentium*, 1964) (*LG*). Looking outwards towards the world the Church lives in produced the Constitution on the Church in the Modern World. (*Gaudium et Spes*, 1965) (*GS*).

During the Council, there were those who fought to retain the status quo of the Church as they knew it. To exempt themselves from the decisions the Council was making, they cited Pope John XXIII's intention that the Council was to be 'pastoral' which they took to mean not binding.[1] (This manner of thinking lives on in the Society of St Pius X). Popes Paul VI, John Paul II and Benedict XVI have all confirmed that the Council is indeed binding on Catholics.[2] The Council was both doctrinal (in the con-

1. For more on this, I recommend Father J Thornhill SM's scholarly reflections on the five-volume history of the Council edited by Alberigo, published in the *Australasian Catholic Record*, July 2005.
2. Any quibble over individual texts within its documents is to be resolved by reference to the aims and teachings of the Council as a whole, and especially its four Constitutions (on the Sacred Liturgy, the Church, Divine Revelation, and the Church in the Modern

tent of its teaching) and pastoral (in the manner of presenting its teaching).

Some commentators described discussions at the Synod for Oceania in 1998 as being 'pastoral', meaning not theologically high-flying. Such a criticism fails to appreciate that the whole purpose of divine revelation is pastoral, that is, 'for us and our salvation'. And, yes, that does make a difference to how God's revelation needs to be presented to people today.

History constantly testifies to the link between pastoral experience and renewal. For example, it was out of his personal journey into the lives of the poor that St Alphonsus de Liguori found the insight and the strength to struggle against rigorist and fear-centred religion.[3]

The Constitution *Gaudium et Spes* was designated a 'Pastoral' Constitution, and continues the link between the renewal of the Church and its pastoral mission.

At the opening of the Council Pope John XXIII memorably taught that the substance of our faith is one thing, and this cannot change; the ways our faith is presented are another; these can change, and ought to for the sake of *effectively communicating* the faith.

The doctrines of faith are not given merely for information. Their purpose is to help draw us into the mystery, the wonder and the joy of salvation. Without change to their meaning, they should be formulated, and reformulated as necessary, to serve that purpose. Paradoxically, it is in making the changes needed for communicating the Church's teachings more effectively that we ensure true continuity between past, present and future. This is because carrying out the Church's mission effectively, and being faithful to the Church's Tradition, are ultimately the same thing.

World), and in continuity with the Church's Tradition. (See *Final Report*, Extraordinary Synod 1985).

3. Those younger priests who are upsetting the faithful with a return to rigorism and legalism might well ask themselves why the Church made St Alphonsus the patron of moral theologians. They could also heed Jesus' challenge to the hard-liners of his day: 'go and learn the meaning of the words: what I want is mercy, not sacrifice' (Matt 9:13). Slavish observance of a system of norms is often an expression of self-concern, and not really Christian; see J Ratzinger, *Introduction to Christianity*, (London: B&O, 1968), 204.

Pre-conciliar catechisms would have served the Catholic people better if they had not allowed the impression to be taken that all Church teachings were equally important and equally certain. This false impression made it more difficult for Catholics to understand that some teachings were in fact less certain, and some less important;[4] and that in areas of the Church's teaching outside the truths of faith, there has sometimes been error and the need for correction. A less defensive Church will not by shy about this. It was not by accident that when dealing with the assent properly due to Church teachings (*LG* 25) the Council omitted from its final draft an earlier phrasing that had echoed the saying: 'Rome has spoken, the matter is closed'.

In a renewed Church, the kind of questioning that properly belongs to adult learning will be not just allowed but encouraged. A sincere commitment to the truth wherever it is to be found, a desire to better understand the faith in the context of living it, and sincere respect for teaching authority within the Church, all presuppose the place of proper questioning, and call for it. It can lead to a better appreciation of the faith.[5]

Catholics would also have been better able to cope with the changes brought about by the Council if we had not had to back-track on our pre-Vatican boast that the Catholic Church never changes and that its liturgy is the same all over the world. This kind of talk too glibly ignored the distinction between what can change and what cannot change.

Sometimes 'the children of this world' recognise the need for change before we do. For example, what can appear to be an abandonment of talk about sin reflects in fact a massive cultural shift which requires new ways of talking about sin. It is the context that has changed. The Church needs to be pro-active in this process to prevent a slide into a morality

4. This needs to be remembered in the context of the Congregation for the Doctrine of the Faith's decision to make the *Catechism of the Catholic Church* 'the authoritative expression of the Catholic faith' to be professed by Anglican groups becoming Catholics.
5. For example, some biblical references to Jesus' sacrifice are not easily distinguished from the pagan idea of sacrificing a victim to appease a vengeful God, and can also give the impression of a cruel Father handing him over for this purpose. The *Catechism of the Catholic Church* (cf 613–616) could have been more sensitive to the sense of revulsion this evokes, and explained that references to our being saved by Jesus' blood are only shorthand for saying we were saved by his faithfulness; his blood (his life) is what it cost him to be faithful. This was the sacrifice that out of love He chose to make.

based on consequences only, and to preserve our tradition's insistence on a morality of the means as well as well as a morality of ends. 'The Church' here includes all who are responsible for theological formation. Theirs is a privileged calling: '... you will shine in the world like bright stars because you are offering it the word of life' (Phil 2:15, 16).

A renewed Church will resist the temptation to absolutise anything that is relative. For example, because the sacraments are actions of Christ, how they are structured and how they are celebrated must be determined by how well they signify—in different cultures and at different times—*what He is still doing*. History shows that the Church has not been afraid to fit them to this need, though it has not always done so in a thoroughgoing manner.

We should note the role of the local churches. When the *Catechism of the Catholic Church* was being promulgated it was explained that the Catechism was not to be regarded as 'the only possible, or even the best way' of articulating the faith (see *L'Osservatore Romano*, 14 April 1993). Nor did adapting it mean merely simplifying or paraphrasing it or drawing conclusions for local application. Rather, the *Catechism of the Catholic Church* was to be 'mediated' by the local Church, that is internalised, discerned, interpreted, and then re-expressed by the local Church for the local Church—always in communion with the other local Churches of the universal Church.

The Church is ill-served by those today who merely repeat documents as they are taken off the internet, as if these did not need to be *mediated* by the local Church under the guidance of its bishop. (Ultimately, the teaching ministry of bishops would be superfluous if it could all be done from the internet.)

Equally, the Church is ill-served by those who cannot see beyond current formulations of Church teaching and laws and practices, as if oblivious of the Church's tradition of debate and of development. Not to see beyond what is, to what might be, is to set the Church up for stagnation and disillusionment.

It is also erroneous to imagine that change must always come from 'the top'. Historically, many significant changes, later adopted by the Church, began in the local churches. Were it otherwise, it might still have been a liturgical 'abuse' for women to read from within the sanctuary and for girls to serve at the altar.

Even in more weighty matters of doctrine, which need the involvement of the pope, his participation has sometimes been by way of *accepting what others have already decided.* J Ratzinger reminds us that

> the first Council of Constantinople, important for the development of the doctrine of the Trinity, convened without representatives of the Western churches, yet became a truly universal Council through the acceptance of its results by Rome and the West . . . It shows that not all initiative in the Church has to rest with the Pope alone . . . (*Theological Highlights*, 114).

A renewed Church will have a stronger sense of what it means to 'mediate' the doctrines and practices of the faith—internalising, interpreting and re-expressing them, and a better appreciation of the role of the local Church in this. And bishops to match.

Letter Nine

Collegiality

Dear bishops,

What the Council taught concerning the relationship between the Bishop of Rome and the other bishops of the Church was really a recovery of ancient Christian belief. And it had huge potential for renewal.

The Council drew an analogy between the unity of St Peter with the other apostles, and the unity of Peter's successors with the bishops of the universal Church. The pope has teaching authority and pastoral governance over the universal Church, and so do the bishops in union with him and under his leadership (cf Dogmatic Constitution of the Church, (*Lumen Gentium*, 1963 (*LG*) 22. It is a collegial responsibility.

Yet opposition to it was strong, and in some quarters acceptance of it is not yet wholehearted. Any serious effort to understand difficulties experienced since the Council needs to look back at the Council debates. Clashes during the Council emanated from deeply entrenched mindsets and different ecclesiologies. These do not change over night.

Explicit opposition from members of the Roman Curia during the Council's debates came not from any kind of perversity, but from a sincere belief that their appointments made them sharers in the special authority of the Pope vis-à-vis the bishops of the world. This would be undermined by the Council's teaching that responsibility for the universal Church comes to all bishops from their episcopal ordination.

Reluctance to fully practise collegiality, by sections of the Roman Curia *since* the Council, has been of a more practical nature, emanating from a fear of losing control, and difficulty trusting the bishops (however, much the right words are always used). It shows itself in centralising practices and persistent efforts at micro-management of the universal Church. It cannot be presumed that this is ill-intentioned. Sincere and dedicated people can act like this out of a genuine concern for the Church, as they see it.

A discussion between a bishop whose diocese in the South Pacific is made up of tiny islands spanning an area of ocean bigger than the whole of Western Europe, and the Cardinal Prefect of one of the Roman Congregations, is illustrative: the bishop had explained that not being able to ordain suitable local married men was preventing him from making Mass available to his people for up to years at a time. He was not questioning the value of celibacy, but he was implying that allowing ordained priesthood to fulfil its fundamental purpose seemed more important than any practices we have attached to it. The Cardinal responded that if ever there was a case for ordaining married men, this was it. But then he added: 'but how would we *control* the situation?' (emphasis mine). One way, of course, would be to entrust that decision to that region's Bishops' Conference.[1]

Bishops are not branch managers who act for a head office. In Catholic ecclesiology their responsibilities in, with and for the local churches is much greater than that. For example, they should not find themselves being told to 'eliminate' a practice before their explanation for it has even been asked for – such as has happened in regard to a practice comparable to ringing the bell at the Consecration.[2]

Bishops, too, can fail to exercise collegial responsibility just by default, or because of excessive obsequiousness. This was not the case, however, when following another disastrous episcopal appointment, the Cardinal

1. What the bishops of that region have been requesting over many years for the sake of their people, the Church now grants in favour of priests who were previously Anglicans.
2. For the New Zealand Maori, hospitality is a sacred duty. They feel most uncomfortable if they have not properly welcomed a guest, especially a distinguished guest. A woman, on behalf of all, calls out their welcome—always out aloud, always dignified and deeply respectful. This call of recognition and welcome is known as the *karanga*. Maori spontaneously desire to affirm the Real Presence of Christ and welcome Him in this way at the Consecration of the Mass. It takes about 10 seconds at each elevation. In the context, it is translatable as 'Come, Lord Jesus', which hardly 'corrupts the liturgical celebration'. To suppress this custom would do real harm.

Archbishop of Vienna felt it necessary to say publicly: 'Once again, we are confronted by occurrences that cause grief and indignation. They make us shake our heads, and seem incomprehensible. And once again the Church has been made to look stupid, and so have we' (reported in *The Tablet*, 21 February 2009). Perhaps Bishops' Conferences should have a greater responsibility for these appointments. This might also help to obviate long delays in filling vacancies that do not accord easily with the Council's teaching on the importance of the bishop's role in the diocese, and of the diocese itself as a portion of God's people entrusted to the care of a bishop.

In the light of the Council's debates, it is hardly surprising that failure to properly respect collegiality has centred around the reform of the liturgy. Archbishop P Marini, Pontifical Master of Ceremonies 1987–2007, has described in detail, on the basis of his own first-hand experience, how after the Council the Congregation for Rites tried to thwart the Council's liturgical reforms. He speaks of

> the tenacious return to pre-conciliar positions, (the) uninterrupted tendency to mistrust the episcopate and its genuine loyalty to the Holy See, and (the) obsessive concern to return to the previous centralisation of all liturgical authority (*A Challenging Reform*, (Collegeville: Liturgical Press, 71); see also 29 ff).

The attitudes described by Marini, both in regard to the liturgy and to collegiality, have persisted into our own day. A case study illustrates the point:

Church law entrusts to Bishops' Conferences the work of preparing translations of the liturgical books, and 'approving' those translations. It pertains to the Congregation for Worship and the Discipline of the Sacraments (CWDS) to 'review' those translations with a view to granting the '*recognitio*' (cf Constitution on the Sacred Liturgy, (*Sacrosanctum Concilium*, 1963 (*SG*) 36; The Decree *Inter Oecumenici*, 1964; and canons 838/2, 838/3).

The Decree *Inter Oecumenici* said the Congregation's role was to 'confirm the decisions of the territorial authorities, and to accede to their proposal and requests' (nn 21–23). The wording of these early documents after the Council reflects how things were intended to be. All this was to change. The separation of functions described above was subverted when the CDWS inserted itself into the work of translating. In order to do this, it demanded the re-configuration of the Commission that had been lawfully constituted by the Bishops' Conferences of the English-speaking world to assist their work.

The Council had encouraged bishops of the same language groups to co-operate internationally (SC 36/3). The Decree implementing the Constitution on the Liturgy, *Inter Oecumenici,* reaffirmed this, while leaving it to the Bishops' Conferences themselves to determine how this would be done. The resulting 'Mixed Commissions' were agencies of the Bishops' Conferences—established and governed by them. They were not established by the Holy See, nor were they agencies of the Holy See. The International Committee for English in the Liturgy (ICEL) was one of these Mixed Commissions.

This arrangement remained in place, accepted and encouraged by the Holy See, for approaching forty years. By the 1990s, English translations, with appropriate adaptations, for thirty of the revised Roman liturgical books had received the *approval* of the Bishops' Conferences and the *recognitio* of the Apostolic See.

The status of Mixed Commissions was peremptorily overturned when in a new Instruction (*Liturgiam Authenticam*, 2002) the Congregation claimed that

- it was for the Holy See to establish Mixed Commissions, at the *request* of the Bishops' Conferences (article 93); (emphasis mine)
- it was for the Holy See to draw up their Statutes ('consulting at least *some* of the bishops involved'), (article 93); (emphasis mine)
- it was the right of the Congregation even to control the appointment of the non-episcopal staff members of the commissions, as well as the way they carry out their work (articles 96, 100);
- 'the Holy See reserved to itself' the right to propose translations in every language, and to approve them for liturgical use (article 104);[3]

3. Of course the Holy See has an ultimate right to do this. The point, however, is what the Holy See has in fact decided to do, as in c 838.

- in effect, the Congregation could do everything itself, setting up its own bodies and by-passing Commissions established by the Bishops' Conferences (article 105); and so on.[4]

A further example of conflict with existing Church law came in the CDWS's *Considerations Pertaining to the Revision of the Statues of the International Commission on English in the Liturgy*, 1999. It gave a directive that 'likewise to be excluded from the activities of the Mixed Commission are relations with commissions or other bodies pertaining to non-Catholic ecclesial communities'. However, the 1993 *Directory for the Application of Principles and Norms on Ecumenism requires* international agencies of Bishops' Conferences to establish structures to ensure an ecumenical dimension to their work (which the Bishops' Conferences had provided for in ICEL's Mandate). The directive countermanding this is in conflict with the 1993 Directory, which is the Church's *existing law* regarding ecumenism.[5]

In October 2003 the Presidents of the English-speaking Bishops' Conferences met in Rome at the invitation of the Cardinal Prefect of the CDWS, for the purpose of facilitating 'understanding and co-operation between the CDWS and the Bishops' Conferences'. The first item on the agenda sent out before the meeting was 'the respective roles and areas of competence of the Congregation and the Bishops' Conferences'.

But a Decree dated 15 September 2003 and published days before the meeting establishing ICEL as a Mixed Commission entirely pre-empted

---

4. On December 18, 2002, the Pontifical Council for the Authentic Interpretation of Legislative Texts declined to adjudicate questions referred to it by the New Zealand Catholic Bishops' Conference on the grounds that the Instruction *Liturgiam Authenticam* was not a legislative text, but concerned 'the manner in which the law is to be put into effect' (c 34). This means, of course, that it lacks binding force if it conflicts with existing Church law (c 34/2). The question of its compatibility with current law, and legitimate custom, was really the point of our enquiry. The Pontifical Council hoped that these issues could be resolved through 'mutual collaboration . . . in a spirit of true ecclesial communion.' (The bishops of ICEL had tried, for over two years, unsuccessfully to meet with the Congregation to discuss the issues.)
5. The Encyclical UUS says that ecumenism 'must pervade all that (the Church) is and does' (n 20).

any meaningful discussion on whether it is the CDWS that establishes Mixed Commissions or the Bishops' Conferences.[6]

The Bishops' Conferences were represented on the new Commission established by the Congregation.

Even apart from the canonical questions arising from the Congregation's interventions, the tone and manner of its actions were in stark contrast to the kind of relationship between the Holy See and Bishops' Conferences presaged in earlier documents; (cf *Pastor Bonus*, article 64/3, 65).

Taking collegiality seriously calls for new ways of exercising the shared responsibility of pope and bishops. The Catholic Church should be seen as a communion of particular (local) churches in communion with the particular (local) church of Rome. At the Council, Patriarch Maximos IV Saigh commented that the Catholic church is too easily perceived instead as the extension of a highly developed particular church (that of Rome) (cf *Commentary on the Documents of Vatican II,* edited by Vorgrimler, Volume 2, 172). That image continues to be an obstacle to Christian unity, and to the practice of collegiality.

Thirty-five years after the Council, Pope John Paul II felt it necessary to say:

> more needs to be done . . . for the reform of the Roman Curia, the organisation of Synods, and the functioning of Episcopal Conferences (Apostolic Letter (*NMI*) 44.)

Some kind of permanent council involving the Pope and the Presidents (or other representatives) of Bishops' Conferences would signify (more effectively than can the Bishops' Synods) that bishops do share with and under the Pope responsibility for the universal Church—by reason of Episcopal Ordination. Part of its role would be to assist the Pope in reviewing and auditing the activities of the Roman Curia.

---

6. Moreover, that first agenda item had disappeared from the agenda paper given us at the meeting, until Cardinal W Napier (South Africa), Archbishop F Carroll (Australia) and I had it restored. But we had decided to just state our position 'for the record', and get on with progressing the work of translating, leaving the resolution of these canonical issues to happier times. I hold correspondence and reports and detailed canonical analysis of this sad saga.

Letter Ten

Re-imagining the Church

Dear people, priests and religious of the diocese,

Before the Council we had inherited a perception and image of the Church that revolved around *ordained ministry* and *religious life*. Clearly, there is no intention here of down-playing the significance of either—quite the opposite. The point I make is this: through what social scientists call 'group bias', the Church came to be perceived primarily in relation to those whose profile in it was more prominent. They were thought of as 'the Church'. It was not uncommon to hear training for the priesthood described as 'joining the Church'.

In this context, the call to holiness seemed to be mainly for Religious and less for others. Responsibility for the mission of the Church seemed to be only for those who were ordained (though they could 'delegate' aspects of it to others who were not). This way of perceiving the Church, whether by religious, priests or laity, is clericalism.

Anyone who might be tempted to think this was rather harmless (or even perhaps something we should return to), should ask themselves: is it really harmless for people to think that some belong to the Church more and some less, depending on whether or not they are ordained? Or that holiness of life is less accessible to those who are not priests or religious? Or that responsibility for the mission of the Church does not come with one's baptism? Is it really harmless to be under the impression that those who are not ordained participate in the Eucharist less than those who are ordained? Is it really Catholic to think that particular callings within the

Church are greater than baptism into Christ? These are the simple misapprehensions of clericalism.[1]

Turning all this around was potentially one of the most far-reaching changes brought about by the Council. It taught that holiness is the calling of *all* the baptised and responsibility for the mission of the Church belongs to *all* the baptised.

It is the sacraments of initiation that are the primary basis of Christian holiness and mission. The greater involvement of lay men and women in decision-making processes (for example, parish and diocesan councils, synods and Marriage Tribunal), in leadership positions and in ministries, in the staffing, management and governance of Catholic schools, in public relations and as spokespersons, in overseas missionary work, and their increased participation in theological, pastoral and spiritual formation, are all manifestations of this teaching being put into practice. The result has been a very real and discernible transition from predominantly clerical ways of thinking about the Church to the broader perspectives that lay women and men have brought to bear on pastoral planning and decision-making, and the presentation of Church teachings. The Church has been greatly enriched by this at parish, diocesan and national levels.[2]

The primacy of our baptismal calling has created a clearer perception of what it means to be the Church. It is already hard to imagine that these activities were carried out almost exclusively by priests and Religious. Pas-

1. Another set of problems occurs when clericalism becomes a culture of power, resulting in excessive deference and lack of accountability. In that context, terrible abuses can more easily go unaddressed. Or even, as the Irish Child Abuse Commission reported (2009) 'the deferential and submissive attitude of the Department of Education towards the Religious Orders compromised its ability to carry out its statutory duty of inspection and monitoring of schools' (see Letter 12).
2. Even these achievements are not the main focus of lay involvement. Ministries and charisms exercised *within the Church* are intended to build up the Church for its mission *in the world*. The Church's mission in the world is the primary arena of the laity's vocation, and the primary arena of their sanctification (see Letter 2). The role of the ordained is to support them for their mission in the world. Both in this way, and through the greater involvement of lay people *within* the Church, the Church itself is being re-imaged.

toral Councils did not even exist.[3] Getting used to it requires what Pope Benedict XVI has called a 'change of mentality', requiring that lay people be viewed no longer just as 'collaborators of the clergy' but truly recognised as 'co-responsible for the Church's being and action', ie for how it looks and what it does. (May 26, 2009, cited on 222.vatican.va)

Perhaps we would all feel more co-responsible for the Church's being and action if co-discipleship received more emphasis than the often-repeated distinction between 'the Church' and 'her sons and daughters', which can seem to put a gap between 'the Church' and ourselves.

New ways of *acting* require and bring about new ways of *relating*: the paternalism, autocracy and dependencies generated by clericalism will have to give way to relationships characterised by dialogue, transparency and accountability, respect and service. After all, 'faith is proposed, not imposed', and 'the Church's teaching office is *at the service of* conscience' (John Paul II, Encyclical *Veritatis Splendor, n.64*).

Addressing a group of US bishops on 12 February 2004, Pope John Paul II spoke of the need for 'a spiritual discernment and critique of certain styles of governance which, even in the name of legitimate concern for good administration and responsible oversight, can run the risk of distancing the pastor from the members of his flock and obscuring his image as their father and brother in Christ'.

Does the Church really need the titles, insignia and sycophantic gestures of obeisance that came to us from the worldly courts of Europe, not from the gospel? (One occasionally hears excuses for these pomposities. But I have never heard one that deals honestly with Jesus' own teaching in Matthew 23:1–10). We have been too slow to ensure that all our practices are consistent with the dignity of personhood and the dignity of Baptism. Does the Church need to offend women—and diminish all of us—by excluding women from roles that do not require the sacramental powers

3. Surprisingly, during one of the New Zealand Bishops' Ad Limina visits in the 1990s, 30 years after we already had parish councils, we were told by an official in one of the Roman Congregations that the Church was 'not yet ready for pastoral councils'!

of ordination?[4] We have been too quick to brand as dissent what is more often a call for honest dialogue and responsible debate. By now we should have learned from the fact that before the Council the Church had to reinstate some of its best theologians who had previously been silenced. Too often Catholics have felt alienated from the Church in ways they do not feel alienated from Christ.

A renewed and re-imaged Church will better reflect the Gospel, and be more careful to avoid practices that people find authoritarian, noncollaborative and oppressive, or lacking in transparency, compassion, humility and joy. In 1 Timothy 5:1, 2, Church leaders are enjoined to respect older men as they would their own father, younger men as brothers, older women as they would their mother, and young women as if they were their sisters.

These new ways of relating require a new way of *thinking*. We need to *think* of the Church as the community of Jesus' disciples, in order for it to *become* like, and *look* like and *function* like, the community of Jesus' disciples, whom he called his mother, sisters and brothers.[5]

To think of the Church in this way is as old as the gospels. To *re-think* of the Church in this way would profile both the attractions and the demands of discipleship. Renewal of the Church requires this re-imaging.

To many of our contemporaries, the Church can seem like a labyrinth of doctrines, laws, duties and customs that are unconnected, imposed and impersonal. Even the realisation that God is somehow 'bigger' than all that can make the Church seem unnecessary. The Church needs an image that is more homely and more personal. Above all, it needs to be an image that highlights the mystery of 'Christ (still) among you' (cf Col 1:27). That *is* the community of his disciples.

---

4. A front page comment in the *L'Osservatore Romano* (10 March 2010) reminds that 'women, both religious and lay, by nature would have been more likely to defend young people in cases of sexual abuse . . . ' and hypothesises that 'a greater female presence, not at a subordinate level, would have been able to rip the veil of masculine secrecy that often covered the denunciation of these misdeeds with silence'.
5. Pope John Paul II often used these images to describe the Church, and all Christians; (cf *The Redeemer of Mankind*, paragraph 21, *That they May be One*, paragraphs 1, 4, 5; *The Lord's Day*, paragraph 4.

If we were living out of that perception of the Church, it would be as unnatural to separate Jesus from his Church as to separate him from his disciples. Our fundamental equality as his disciples would take precedence over all other differences. Our relationship to Him would constitute the calling of every disciple to holiness—not some more than others. Those whose sense of failure can make them feel disqualified from a community perceived as respectable can feel at home in a community to which 'tax collectors and sinners' were the first to be called.

The teachings and practices of our faith would not be experienced as extraneous and imposed; they would be the things we want to say and do together because of Christ among us. Practising the faith would not be perceived as a private, individual affair separate from daily life (cf Pastoral Constitution on the Church in the Modern World (*Gaudium et Spes*), (*GS*) n 43) because discipleship cannot be part-time. Evangelisation would emanate from the desire to talk about the One we have discovered and the difference He makes.

This re-imaging of the Church does not put present-day experience above faith; it enhances the 'signs of credibility' needed for faith.

Letter Eleven

Religious Life and Priesthood

Dear people, priests and religious of the diocese,

In my previous letter I highlighted the Council's teaching on the call of all the baptised to holiness and on the responsibility of all the baptised for the mission of the Church. I am writing now to explain how this does not diminish the significance of priesthood and religious life.

In fact, the opposite is true: unburdened by the assumptions and expectations of clericalism, the true significance of ordained priesthood is more easily identified, appreciated and affirmed. And when the universal call to holiness is recognised, it becomes clearer that professed Religious have a message for all of us.

If it is good for the Church not to be narrowly equated with priesthood and religious life, it is also good for priesthood and religious life. The 'massive shift in how the Church is perceived' becomes a new and healthier seedbed for vocations, including vocations to priesthood and religious life. Gradually, vocations will be less motivated by clericalism's misapprehensions regarding how holiness, mission, belonging and participation are to be understood. During the time it takes for the Church to make the transition, it could be expected that there would be a lag in new vocations, and that some of those coming forward would still be clinging to the trappings of clericalism. But because the re-imaging of the Church is the work of the Holy Spirit acting through a General Council, a faith-filled response looks forward with expectation to the vocations that will emerge from it.

In a renewed, ie more Christ-centred Church, how people serve will be conditioned more by how they love. Love tends to reciprocate even the manner of the other's loving. Jesus gave his all; reciprocated love gives all.

Some of this loving will have the characteristics of 'excess'. Paul Tillich, speaking of the woman who broke the jar of precious ointment to anoint Jesus' feet against the reasonable objections of his disciples, suggests that she represents the 'unreasonable' factor in the loving of those who have been struck by the realisation of how extraordinary God's love for us really is. The *appropriate* response to excessive love is 'excessive' love. People in love do mad things! This love breaks conventions (cf the father of the prodigal son), and cannot be reduced to measured, careful, sensible, 'sufficient', 'normal' ways of loving.

Religious life is not alone in this, but it does come out of this kind of loving, and serves as a sign that we *all* called to love God 'above all things'.

Only great love—knowing how much we have all been loved and loving in return—will be strong enough to draw men and women to vocations that are sharply counter-cultural; vocations that call for celibacy within a highly sexualised culture; detachment from accumulating wealth within a culture dedicated to possessions; a long period of formation and limited career progression within a culture that is 'instant' and associates success with position and status. The tide against us is strong. But we are in the boat with Him who can quieten the storms around us and within us.

Young people looking for more generous and idealistic ways of serving Christ will be more likely to look for ways of serving that go beyond the limits of what seems ordinary, sufficient and sensible. In a renewed Church, our loving will come more from the realisation of how much we have been loved. In this context, celibacy will be more willingly chosen, and by the rest of the Church more willingly supported. Again, the renewal of the Church comes back to *deeper relationships* with the person of Jesus Christ.

It is a mistake to think that Jesus handed over to others to carry on where he left off. He has never left off. Those who are ordained to act in his name only give voice to what he himself is still doing.

> There is only one Pastor of the Church and he is Jesus Christ, the Good Shepherd. All that priests do as pastors is serve Christ's own pastoring of the Church. There is only one priest in the Church, Jesus Christ, and all that Christian priests do is to be the sacramental presence of Christ's own priesthood. There is only one Teacher of the Church, Jesus Christ, and all that priests do is give voice to Jesus who speaks through them as the Word of life for their hearers. As priests preside over the Church's liturgy and over the Christian community, they do so only as servants of Christ who alone is head of the Church. (Bishop Michael Putney, Foreword in *The Prayer of the Priest*, William F Ekert, (Arizonia: Medio Media, 2005).

These images (High Priest, Good Shepherd, Head of his Body) describe Christ's relationship to all of us who are the Church. We are the Church only to the extent that we *receive* our life from Christ. The ordained ministry of word and sacrament symbolises this relationship of *receiving* from Christ. That is the service ordained ministries perform. And their authority to do this is also *received*—in the sacrament of Holy Orders.

It is an authority that is best described in terms of holiness. The Ordination rites (especially those of the third, fifth and seventh centuries) asked for the ordinand's 'deep inner renewal' for the sake of his ministry to others. His own renewal was integral to the exercise of his ministry. (cf D Power OMI, *Ministers of Christ and His Church*, [London: Chapman, 1969], 60, 61 & 122.) Priestly 'spirituality' is the ongoing work of bringing about this convergence between his call to holiness and his call to ministry.

Priests are in a unique position to spoil renewal for everyone just by opting for the routines of maintenance mode—within a Church whose very nature is *mission*. Staying in, or getting back into, *mission mode* involves ongoing conversion, and that continuing 'human, spiritual, intellectual and pastoral formation' which Pope John Paul II described cogently as

> a requirement of the priest's own faithfulness to his ministry and to his very being. It is love for Jesus Christ and fidelity to oneself. But it is also an *act of love for the people of God*, at whose service the priest is placed. Indeed, an act of *true and proper justice*: the priest owes it to God's people . . . Ongoing formation is necessary to ensure that the priest can properly respond to this right of the

People of God. (On The formation of Priests in Today's Circumstances (*Pastores Dabo Vobis*, 1992) (*PDV*) 70). (Pope John Paul II's own emphases).

Letter Twelve

Abuse—Of People and Power

Dear Father,

Like many other faithful priests you have felt hurt by the way you are being tarred with the same brush as those who have done terrible harm by sexual offending, to say nothing of the harm also done by the Church's inadequate responses, and mismanagement of it. Relentless media reporting seems to make us all guilty, at least by association. Might it help to remember that this same clamour of the media must seem like relief and vindication to those who have been unheard, disbelieved and ignored for so long? We might even ask ourselves whether they would have had redress at all were it not for the media. So, for the victims' sake, let us bear what we must bear, and trust the good sense of people to know that when individuals let their families down, it is not the whole family that is guilty.

This does not mean, of course, that we may just ride out the storm in the expectation of returning to 'normal'. On the contrary, from being a Church in which so much could go so wrong for so long, we need to become a Church that can never be like that again. They badly miss the point who want to go back to the more regimented life-styles and more repressive methods of formation of any earlier time. Most of the sexual offending we are dealing with today came out of that kind of environment.

The kind of changes that are needed come into focus more clearly when we see with the eyes of the victims, including many who have been too badly damaged to care whether the Church is renewed or not. If there is paradox here, it is the paradox prefigured in the gospel: those who put the Church's reputation ahead of the safety of children and youth have ruined its reputation; the Church's true face has always been seen in those who put the needs of others—especially the most vulnerable—ahead of their own. The need is for radical com-passion, that is, suffering-with those who have been deeply humiliated, betrayed, and psychologically/emotionally maimed for life. There is a point at which renewal, conversion and compassion are the same thing.

> The empathic stance demands that we put our own needs for understanding aside and focus steadfastly on the needs of the other. It will be our own unflinching love and compassion in the face of hostility and hurt that will play a large part in the healing of those wounded by abuse and that eventually may include forgiveness. Something profound has happened that has rent the fabric of our relationships. Trust has been damaged and we cannot return to the place we began. Perhaps over some decades, trust can be rebuilt and new relationships forged. (Catherine Shelton rsj (MA); private correspondence).

The offenders, of course, have already seen the frightened eyes of their victims and it has not deterred them. This says something about the depths of the pathology affecting them. Many of them hated what they were doing, and experienced their obsession as a terrible burden. Yes, compassion must extend to them too.

Before the obsessive/compulsive nature of paedophilia was generally understood, bishops—like most people—thought of it as wrong-doing that the culprits could put a stop to.[1] And so they believed, wrongly but in good faith, that appropriate admonitions and spiritual direction could effectively prevent further offending.

> The great majority of these cases go back to the 1960s and 1970s, when bishops often regarded sexual abuse as a sin rather than also a pathological condition, and when lawyers and psychologists often reassured them that it was safe to re-assign priests after treatment (Timothy Radcliffe OP, *The Tablet*, 10 April 2010, 4).

How wrong we all were. Those who made this mistake, albeit in good faith, also experience a burden and great sorrow. If ever there was an issue that has engendered deep mistrust of the Church and a sense of betrayal,

1. It has been compared to alcoholism, both as an illness and as a misunderstood illness, as when it was commonly believed that the alcoholic could stop drinking by choosing to stop.

it has been the sexual abuse issue and especially the mishandling of it. I refuse to tar all bishops with the same brush because I know how well some have handled it. But it has to be said that we bishops have been part of an ecclesiastical culture that too easily led to this matter being dealt with ineptly and unjustly.

The experience of human brokenness and failure will be more of a challenge to any who cling to the misconception that holiness somehow belongs more to the institutional life of the Church. For *all of us* holiness depends entirely on our relationship with Christ in whatever circumstances of life (see Letter 10). Sinfulness—for all of us—is the condition of being away from where we most need to be. The scriptures depict this self-alienation as living in exile and in the desert where we learn the meaning of our unfaithfulness, and rediscover the wonder of God's mercy. Through this crisis we could rediscover the Church's identity as the community of redeemed sinners, reconciled and reconciling (cf 2 Cor 5:17–20).

The need to focus on the rights of victims has made us wary of speaking about forgiveness. We want to avoid language that might be mistaken for leniency or cheap grace. We also want to respect victims' own pace in the journey back to wholeness. Their deepest needs must first be met, including the need to know they have been believed (this is necessary for their healing), and that every appropriate step is being taken to ensure the offender will not commit the same crimes against others. This is primarily a matter of attitudes, but also of structures.[2]

But they also need to experience hope, which presupposes the possibility of moving on. Anger, hurt and mistrust are appropriate responses to the outrage of sexual abuse and the further outrage of being left without redress. But these emotions must be seen as a stage on a journey. Health professionals who speak about stress remind us that strong emotions,

2. In 1993, after two years preparation, formal protocols for dealing with sexual abuse by priests and religious were adopted by the six dioceses and religious orders of New Zealand, and a Protocol Committee established in each diocese. In 1998 *A Path to Healing* was published (revised in 2001 and 2010). In 2002 the New Zealand Bishops issued a pastoral letter apologising to victims and to the Catholic people for abuse by clergy (Catholic.org.nz). In 2004 a National Office of Professional Standards was established to review cases handled by Protocol Committees. From the time the problem emerged in 1992, the Church has supported complainants in taking their cases to the Police if criminal offending was involved.

such as hostility, cause biochemical changes in us, and that sometimes these can cause or aggravate disease. They also point out that the inability to forgive can be a significant stress factor in the life of the one who is unable to forgive. In other words, they are telling us that the deepest healing comes with forgiving. This is not an easy journey, and victims need to experience a lot of love before it can happen. No time-frame can be imposed for forgiveness, but nor can we be indifferent to whether or not it happens. To love, unobtrusively and non-judgmentally, is the calling of the community to which the offender belonged. Otherwise the community is not participating in its own renewal.

Having said we must bear with the way the media are reporting these matters, it is in order also to say that the media need to face up to what they are doing: the abuse of children is widespread in every part of society, and so to make it look like a Catholic Church problem is tantamount to another form of cover-up. According to Ronald Rolheiser OMI, (*On Carrying a Scandal Biblically*, www.ronaldrolheiser.com/articles), sexual abuse is so widespread in the USA that priests represent less than 1% of the problem.[3]

This does not excuse any of our own offending. In a sense, ours is worse because of the sacred ministry entrusted to us.

> Acknowledgment of the inherent power imbalance in fiduciary relationships is essential. Even if an individual priest does not feel as if he has much personal power, especially now, not to acknowledge the power of his role can be self-deceptive. He puts himself at risk when he minimises the magnitude of his power. Abuse surely does occur elsewhere in society, but the intensified impact of abuse and the devastating betrayal experienced when abuse is in the context of a spiritual relationship go to the very soul of a person and his/her relationship with God. The fiduciary relationship is shattered;

3. The point matters because 'the whole truth' matters. Professionals who have worked with paedophiles over many years in Britain report that the vast majority are not celibates, and most are not Catholics. A Jewish commentator on the situation in the USA (Sam Millar) reports on a survey showing a significantly higher incidence among Protestant ministers than Catholic priests. Other statistics show there is no correlation between paedophilia and celibacy, and that most sexual abuse occurs within family homes, even if not always by blood relatives. My concern in this letter has been with our own renewal.

> belief in the very goodness of God, humanity and the universe is fractured. (Sr Catherine Shelton rsj).

When discussing the causes of contemporary atheism, the Second Vatican Council spoke of the responsibility believers themselves have to bear for ways of living that 'conceal rather than reveal the authentic face of God and religion' (Pastoral Constitution on the Church in the Modern World, *Gaudium et Spes, 1965,*) (*GS*) 19. Recent scandals are, at least in that sense, more of the same. Now, more than ever, we need to keep on doing the kind of things we would like the Church to be remembered for.

You yourself are doing that by continuing your practice of being present to children out in the school play grounds. Keeping a distance from them because of what people might think was an understandable reaction, but an over-reaction. Children need to experience the world around them as a friendly place, not one in which they have to hold most people in suspicion. That harms them in another way. By not putting your own reputation and the risk of being misjudged ahead of the children's needs, you are helping to restore the Church's rightful reputation.

And if you are judged unfairly, that becomes an opening for the most radical kind of renewal. On Good Friday (which wasn't fair, either) not only was evil about to be defeated, it was being seconded into the dynamics of its own defeat. Something like this happens when we take the evils that come our way and give back good: 'do good to those who persecute you, bless those who curse you, pray for those who abuse you . . . ' (cf Lk 6:27–31, Rom 12:14). Renewal enters the world in this way too.

Letter Thirteen

Initiation into the Church

Dear parents and parishioners involved in preparing candidates for sacraments of initiation,

The renewal of the Church requires renewal at the point of entry. Initiation into the Church has become too routine and conventional. It needs to reflect better the dramatic reality of what is happening. Initiation is, after all, about being 'born again' through a 'baptism with the Holy Spirit'. It was for this that Christ came (Jn 1:33, 34). This pouring out of the Holy Spirit had been foretold by the prophets (for example Ezech 36:25–27; Jl 3:1–2;) and was to be fulfilled after Jesus' resurrection (Acts 1:4–5; 2:33). New life would flow as from 'fountains of living water' (Jn 7:38–39). Our pastoral and liturgical practices need to echo the drama of what we are being initiated into. The Church herself is being made new.

A heightened awareness of what initiation really means can only come about by enhancing the process of preparation for it. This is why the catechumenate is so important. It originated from the need to better prepare candidates and to prevent reception into the Church from being taken too lightly.

The origins of the catechumenate are also an example of how the Church *adapts its liturgical rites to meet its pastoral needs.* Until about the year 180 AD, the Christian community's rites of initiation did not take the form of a structured process. But between the years 180 to 300 AD, the risk of converts falling away because of heresy or persecution created the need for a more structured process, namely the catechumenate. This preparatory period could last for as long as three years, and led to an intense, final preparation that culminated in the Easter vigil. The Church had adapted its liturgical rites to meet its pastoral needs.

Later, when the needs changed, so did the Church's response. During the reign of Constantine, persecution was no longer the danger; becoming a Christian had become socially acceptable and even beneficial. Now, many joined the Church, but their conversion was not always deep. They were at risk of falling away for that reason. What was easily come by was easily abandoned. So the Church developed the Lenten season further and made of it a brief but intense catechumenate. The Easter vigil was also further developed, and the fifty days after Easter became a time of great joy and a time for depthing the new Christians' understanding of what had happened. This is what was restored to the Church when in 1972 the new Rite for the Christian Initiation of Adults was promulgated by Pope Paul VI.

It is essentially a journey of evangelisation, personal conversion and catechesis. It takes time; it is structured around stages and the crossing of thresholds, and it gives candidates an experience of Christian life and Christian community. Most importantly, it is rooted in the liturgical seasons of Lent and Easter. At Easter the sacraments of initiation are celebrated and initiation is complete.[1] This is the paradigm of Christian initiation. It is normative for adults and young people of catechetical age who are not already baptised.

The Confirmation of those who *were baptised as infants* also needs to be put into the context of the Church's pastoral needs. They were pastoral/theological considerations that first led to Confirmation being separated from Baptism. (Deferring Confirmation until the visit of the bishop highlighted the relationship with the bishop entered into through initiation into the Church.) Likewise they were pastoral reasons that led Pope St Pius X to bring first Holy Communion forward to around the age of discretion. The Church can do that with its sacraments; sacraments, like the Sabbath, are for us, not we for them.[2]

1. As far as possible, baptisms that are not celebrated at Easter should be celebrated on Sundays because every Sunday is an echo of Easter Sunday. In this way, baptism is still being linked to the liturgical year.
2. Even when Confirmation comes after first Holy Communion, the paramountcy of Eucharist is being affirmed by the Church's practice of 'anticipating'—as if the Church

Those who would insist on the order—Baptism-Confirmation-Eucharist for children are following the paradigm of Christian initiation to that extent; but not to the extent that the paradigm also involves a journey of evangelisation, personal conversion and catechesis, and connections with the liturgical seasons. Even allowing for the fact that this journey continues after full initiation, in today's circumstances the journey seems especially important *as part of the preparation.* Whichever order is chosen (Confirmation before or after first Holy Communion) some departure from the paradigm is involved. In my view, modifying the order is less consequential than diminishing the journey. Besides, the witness given by mid to late teenagers stepping forward for the sacrament of Confirmation can be very moving, and memorable for themselves and for all who see it to an extent that is not noticeable at Confirmation for children.

Some commentators overdraw the contrast between the candidates' faith 'commitment' (which is how they describe adolescent Confirmation), and 'celebrating the Gift of the Holy Spirit' (which is how they describe infant and adult Confirmation). At whatever age, Confirmation is *always* a sacrament of initiation (it cannot be anything else), and is always more about God's commitment to us than ours to God.[3]

I can understand those who worry that when Confirmation is left until the teen years, fewer come forward. But this concern needs to be seen against a wider background. Fifty years ago, Karl Rahner predicted that as the Western world became more secular, religious practice would depend less on convention and more on conviction; members would be fewer, but more committed. This is precisely what has been happening. Secularism itself is forcing us to be counter-cultural. That is the context in which we initiate people for mission. In that context, do we, for the sake of confirming greater numbers opt for a younger age (knowing, however, that this will not guarantee sustained practice); or do we, for the sake of a more committed, more counter-cultural membership, wait until candidates are

---

were saying: even though you are still preparing for Confirmation, we can't wait for you to receive the Bread of Life (somewhat as the Eastern churches cannot wait even until the age of discretion).

3. Since 'grace builds on nature', I wonder what might result from bringing into consideration the idea of *participation* as it is understood in Catholic social teaching. In feudal societies it was more acceptable for people's decisions to be made for them (as we still do for children); today we more readily acknowledge the right of people to participate, so far as possible, in the decisions that will affect their lives.

ready to look for goals and purpose in their lives (knowing that some will have already dropped out)?

This decision should not be made in isolation from the meaning of the sacrament. Participation in the life and mission of the Church means being disciples and witnesses of Jesus. The *Catechism of the Catholic Church* makes it clear that candidates for Confirmation must be 'prepared to assume the role of disciple and witness to Christ both within the ecclesial community and in temporal affairs' (cf n1319). Today this means being counter-cultural, and it will appeal to them only if they are developing a personal relationship with Him and beginning to experience for themselves the attraction of His companionship.

Their fundamental preparation for Confirmation comes about through *experiencing* the life and mission of the Church and being attracted to it. This happens through experiencing the Church's prayer life, its journey through the liturgical seasons, its exposure to the Lectionary, its rituals and symbols, its apostolates, and the various ways the Catholic community reaches out to people in any kind of need. After all, this is—for *all* of us—where the Christian faith becomes real. Candidates need to see their parents and other parishioners finding fulfilment in doing these things. They need to discover incentives for moving from 'having to be' confirmed to 'wanting to be' confirmed.

Experiencing the life and mission of the Church calls for some understanding of it. Experience without understanding is fluid and shapeless. It is not good enough to 'have the experience and miss the meaning.' The understanding called for is not just knowing Church teachings, or knowing *about* God. It is more like having one's eyes opened to a wonderful plan God had in mind before the world was made and that includes one's self and everyone else. (This is the ultimate in 'belonging').

That plan unfolded first in the work of creating, then in human history, and now—in a privileged way—in the liturgy. Together, these make up what is called 'salvation history.'[4] It is this overarching narrative of *what*

4. St Augustine used to require candidates to be given 'the whole account of God's intervention in human history that would later be unfolded for them in liturgical worship for the rest of their lives….' (Catherine Dooley, in *Issues in the Christian Initiation of Children*, Ed. Kathy Brown, Frank Sokol Chicago 1989, p 53)

God is doing that gives coherence to what otherwise appear to be disconnected religious doctrines. Preparation for Confirmation is much more than a narrow, individualistic focus on 'the gifts of the Holy Spirit'.

But what God is doing—'out there'—needs to connect with what God is doing in human hearts. The longings of the human heart (and corresponding fears) are *intimations* of what we are made for. God's deeds in human history (recorded in the Jewish and Christian scriptures) *confirm* that our deepest longings are destined to be fulfilled. And in the liturgy we become personally *involved* in what God is doing.

Within the limits of what young people can manage, and making allowance for different personality types, we should not be afraid to challenge candidates over what it means to be disciples and witnesses. Why should they believe that getting involved in the life and mission of the Church is important if initiation into it requires little of them? Getting secular qualifications requires of them a certain amount of study and reading, and preparation over a period of time. On what grounds would we expect less of them when it comes to preparing them to participate more fully in the life and mission of the Church?

Sometimes the problem is the indifference of parents, who in turn were probably confirmed without very much being asked of them. If we have been asking too little, the solution is not to ask less.

Preparation for Confirmation involves providing for candidates what was not provided for them at their infant baptism, and won't be provided for them through initiation as adults.

This suggests a significant lacuna in the Church's present pastoral/liturgical practices. This gap is not addressed by Confirmation 'programmes' that don't require some commitment to the journey of evangelisation, personal conversion and catechesis. Nor does religious education fill the gap because it is an entirely different process (cf *General Catechetical Directory*, nn 65, 66, 73). Much less should preparation for Confirmation seem like a school subject. Confirmation is *an event in the life of the parish* which the school is rightly part of, with a role to play. School staff are often the best equipped to help, and better able to involve parents, including non-practising and non-Catholic parents. But the candidates preparing for sacraments of initiation are doing so *as parishioners*.

The age for Confirmation is not primarily chronological. It is determined by the answer to the question: Are they ready? Readiness may vary from parish to parish because it depends on the dispositions of the candidates themselves, the influence of their friends, the faith-practice of their families, and how the parishes themselves involve them in suitable apostolates or ministries. If candidates must be 'prepared to assume the role of disciple and witness . . .' (*Catechism*, n 1319), then perhaps it is the parish itself that is 'not ready' if it does not provide opportunities to involve them as disciples and witnesses, in ways proportionate to their years. Lack of follow-up to Confirmation is part of the overall problem. As readiness may vary from parish to parish, so may age.

Their preparation can be linked to the liturgical seasons by running their preparation through Lent, concurrently with the RCIA, but going beyond Easter to Pentecost, given its focus on mission and witness.

Letter Fourteen

Liturgical Renewal

Dear brother priests,

Could there be any greater privilege, and reason for humility, than the part Christ gives us in the celebration of the sacraments and liturgy. Here we experience some of our clearest glimpses of Christ in the midst of His people. (See The Constitution on the Sacred Liturgy, *Sacrosanctum Concilium*, 1963 (*SC*) 7.)

For a deeper appreciation of the mysteries we celebrate, I refer you to the General Instruction of the Roman Missal (GIRM), The Introduction to the Lectionary, The Introduction to the Rite for the Christian Initiation of Adults (RCIA) and the Introductions to each of the sacraments. My focus in this letter is on our leadership.

The need at this time is for good leadership at every level. Leadership does not come from those who would like all their thinking to have been done for them. What I offer you here is rather a *way of thinking* that might assist your leadership. I shall do this under eight headings.

(i) Renewal *through* the liturgy

In the early years of the twentieth century, Pope St Pius X had wanted to shore up the Christian faith against perceptions that scientific thought and historical-critical methods would bring about the end of religious beliefs and practices.

> But when he looked at his resources in the Church, he saw the vast majority of Catholics subsisting on a diet of sentimental piety and engaging in devotions that were peripheral to the central myster-

> ies of faith… he had become convinced that this sort of religiosity would never enable the Church to withstand the grave spiritual and cultural crisis of the times. A Church whose membership lived on forms of piety that were themselves deeply imbued with the spirit and tastes of the age was ill-equipped to reassert its own identity in a secularised and secularising world. (Mark Searle, *Called to Participate*, edited by Barbara Searle & Anne Koester [Collegeville: Liturgical Press, 2006], 5).

Private devotions play an important part in intensifying our relationship with God. Liturgy, however, does more: it enables us to transcend the narrow horizons of our own concerns, moods, gratifications, preferences and comfort-zones. It draws us into union with the Body that was broken and 'given up' for others, and the Blood that was 'poured out' for others. In other words, we come to *participate* in something bigger than ourselves. It was Pope St Pius X who first called for 'active participation in the most sacred mysteries and in the public and solemn prayer of the Church' (Motu proprio, *Tra le sollecitudini*, 1903).

Pope John XXIII's reason for convening the Second Vatican Council was also to better fit the Church for its mission in the world today. In the first paragraph of its first document, it linked the renewal of the Church with the renewal of the liturgy (*SC* 1).

As it affects the celebration of Eucharist, the liturgical renewal involves the revision of the Roman Missal (including a Lectionary with its wider selection of scripture readings), the translation of the Missal into the vernacular languages, and the re-ordering and refurbishing of churches—all intended to facilitate that 'full, conscious and active participation in liturgical celebrations which is demanded by *the very nature of the liturgy*' (*SC* 14, emphasis added).

(ii) 'Full, conscious and active participation'

It is perhaps understandable, though unfortunate, that 'full, conscious and active participation' has too often been thought of only as our joining in the words, actions and roles of the liturgy; in other words, participation in the *rite*. This limited understanding of 'participation' also lends itself to attempts at making the liturgy more 'relevant' to particular agendas; but this is only another way of not thinking past the words and actions *of the rite.*[1]

We need to look beyond the words, actions and roles of the rite to what the rite itself ultimately signifies. There is, after all, only one Liturgy; it took place at one point in the history of the world: the death and resurrection of Christ. That is what the celebration of Eucharist *makes present* to us, and *draws us into*. That is the Event, or Mystery—beyond the rite itself—that we *participate in*. Through the power of the Holy Spirit we become united to Christ's offering of himself to the Father. The readings, chants, symbols and silences of the rite help us to become caught up in it and surrender ourselves to it. In this way our participation is a *contemplative* experience.

In union with Christ and with one another, we enter the sanctuary of God's presence and are transformed by the experience. We come out of that experience empowered to 'live no longer for ourselves but for Him' (cf Eucharistic Prayer IV).[2] The Eastern churches have a strong sense of the liturgy taking place simultaneously in heaven and on earth. In the Roman Rite, too, 'we join the angels and saints in their song of joy' (Prefaces).

And so liturgy looks beyond appearances to the deepest meaning of history and to what God is doing in the world. To put us in touch with the deep flow of 'salvation history' it needs to be a time that is countercultural to all that keeps us on the surface of life. It can ill afford to be just another experience of busyness, noise and wordiness, pressures and banalities. Ongoing renewal requires that our manner of participating in the rites lead more surely to our participation in the Mystery: 'The Mystery is Christ among you, your hope of glory' (Col 1:27).[3]

1. The English translation 'active participation' has contributed to that limited understanding of participation. What the Council was restoring by its reference to '*consciam atque actuosam . . . participationem*' and '*plena participatio*' was actual engagement by the whole congregation in the liturgy itself, as distinct from merely being 'present at' or 'assisting at' the liturgy, or using it as a time for private devotion.
2. It has been suggested that instead of talking about 'liturgy planning' we should talk about 'preparing for liturgy' (Austin Fleming, quoted by Searle, 13).
3. Presiding ministers need to know how to preside without drawing attention to themselves, but rather drawing the congregation, including themselves, into the mystery; with warmth, however, and not mechanically. Similarly with the Sign of Peace: it is not a greeting (for which the proper place would have been before Mass began) and

(iii) What the Council said—re renewing the rites

Simplistic interpretations of the Council have no future, not only because they are rightly rebuked, but also because it is the Council that has a future. The Council remains paramount, and all post-conciliar Instructions, even those issued by the Holy See, are intended to be interpreted in the light of the Council's own teaching and by reference to it. They are not intended to 'correct' the Council. The Council taught that

> The rite of Mass is to be revised in such a way that the intrinsic nature and purpose of its several parts, as well as the connection between them, may be more clearly manifested, and that devout and active participation by the faithful may be more easily achieved.
>
> For this purpose the rites are to be simplified, due care being taken to preserve their substance. Parts which with the passage of time came to be duplicated, or were added with little advantage, are to be omitted. Other parts which suffered loss through accidents of history are to be restored to the vigour they had in the days of the Holy Fathers, as may seem useful or necessary (50).

Having distinguished between 'unchangeable elements divinely instituted' and 'elements subject to change', the Council said that

> These latter not only may be changed but ought to be changed if with the passage of time they have suffered from the intrusion of anything out of harmony with the inner nature of the liturgy or have become less suitable. In this restoration both texts and rites should be drawn up so as to express more clearly the holy things which they signify. The Christian people, as far as is possible, should be able to understand them with ease and take part in them fully, actively, and as a community (21).
>
> Provided the substantial unity of the Roman Rite is maintained, the revision of liturgical books should allow for legitimate varia-

---

therefore is not carried out in the way we express a greeting. (Nor is it a sign of reconciliation which would have been located before we take our gifts to the altar.) Instead, it is located at that sacred moment when we are preparing to receive the Sacrament. It reminds us that Christ whom we receive in the sacrament is also present in the person of our neighbour. It, too, is celebrating the mystery of 'Christ among you'. And so it is carried out in a spirit of *deep reverence*.

> tions and adaptations to different groups, regions, and peoples, especially in mission lands. Where opportune, the same applies to the structuring of rites and the devising of rubrics (38).

The Council took care to preserve and draw from the Church's most authentic Tradition.

Further, the 1962 Missal contained only an extremely limited selection of scripture readings, and so the Council taught that

> The treasures of the Bible are to be opened up more lavishly, so that richer fare may be provided for the faithful at the table of God's Word. In this way a more representative portion of the holy Scriptures will be read to the people over a set cycle of years (51).

Any claim that the liturgical reform was not necessary would be in conflict with these decisions of the Council. The extended use of the 1962 Missal, therefore, can only be regarded as a concession to special needs.

(iv) The meaning of concessions

In recent times, the Holy See has allowed a return to some of the practices that were in place before the reform of the liturgy—both because of some people's attachment to previous practices, and because of some people's difficulties in adapting to change. These allowances are to be seen as pastorally motivated *concessions*. The revised liturgy is still the norm. When restoring the 1962 Missal, Pope Benedict explained that the Missal promulgated by Pope Paul VI was still, both juridically and in practice, the 'ordinary' form of the Roman rite. He also described it as the 'normal' form of the Eucharistic liturgy (cf *Motu Proprio Summorum Pontificum*, 2007). There is 'no contradiction' (Pope Benedict XVI) between the two forms only so long as the distinction between ordinary and extraordinary is honoured in practice. They betray the pope's intentions who promote the 1962 Missal as it were another ordinary form of the Roman Rite. The two Missals can never be on an equal footing because that would mean the Church has one Missal based on the Council's teaching that reform was necessary, and another based on the supposition that reform was not necessary! That *would be* a contradiction. The Council taught that reform *was necessary*, and so the extended use of the previous Missal can only be a *concession* for the benefit any 'stable group' of the faithful who are attached to the 1962 Missal. It is not about recruiting Catholics to that form of the Mass. The pope did not intend this concession to be used in support of claims that earlier practices were 'better', or that the liturgical reform was a 'mistake', or that the 1962 Missal is to eventually replace the revised Missal.[4]

Nor was the pope granting an exemption to any Catholics, priests or people, from their other Catholic obligations. One of these other obligations is liturgical formation. We are all obliged to learn more about the Church's teaching concerning the liturgy. This includes studying the Council's teachings and the current General Instruction of the Roman Missal. Ultimately, liturgy is not about personal preferences and attachments.

The other obligations from which Catholics cannot claim exemption are the apostolates and pastoral activities of their parish, including the Church's work for social justice and for Christian unity. Too often the preference for the extraordinary form is but part of an individualistic piety and clericalist ecclesiology (see Letter 11 on *Re-imaging the Church*).

(v) Liturgical catechesis

Adaptations of the liturgy prepared by Bishops' Conferences must be in accordance with the 'meaning and character of each part of the celebration' (General Instruction of the Roman Missal, 2003 (*GIRM*) 43). This gives us a touchstone for sound liturgical catechesis. Good catechesis aims to ensure that priests' and people's actions and responses correspond in the best possible way to the 'meaning and character of each part of the celebration'.[5] By means of the hymns, responses, silences, postures and

4. Rejecting the pastoral judgements of a General Council that has been endorsed by every Pope since is not the Catholic way. Those who are using Pope Benedict's *Motu proprio* as a tool for reversing the liturgical reform are obsessed by their own perception of a dichotomy between the worship of God and the dynamics of Christian community. They risk accentuating the deadly dualism discussed in Letter 2. The real need is to implement 'full, active and conscious participation' in a truly contemplative way.
5. It is to be expected that catechesis based on the meaning of the rite will involve some conflict with concessions that are based on other considerations. The concession to kneel during the whole Eucharistic Prayer is a case in point. This is a practice that developed in some countries when people's focus was mainly on devotion to the real

gestures, we express—with our whole self—what we believe is happening at each part of the liturgy. They embody our faith.

Liturgical catechesis also needs to bring home to parishioners the relationship between Church architecture and the nature of the liturgy. Church architecture and furnishings should feature the ways that Christ is present in the celebration of Eucharist. Altar, ambo, chair and body of the church are in a dynamic relationship with each other, highlighting Christ's presence in the Sacrament, the Word, the priest and the congregation.

In addition, the baptismal waters should be located where they symbolise entry into this community; the Tabernacle located in a place suitable for private devotion outside of the liturgy; and the musicians where they can lead the congregation's participation in the singing. The different spaces and sites within the building are all in the service of 'full, conscious and active participation'; (see Appendix I).

So, too, is liturgical music. It must deepen our awareness of what is happening, and draw us into it. Otherwise it doesn't belong.

> . . . everything—texts, music, execution—ought to correspond to the meaning of the mystery being celebrated, the structure of the rite, and the liturgical seasons (Benedict XVI, Post-Synodal Exhortation On the Eucharist as the Source and Summit of the Church's Life and Mission, *Sacramentum Caritatis*, 2007 (*SC*) 42).

Increasingly, liturgical catechesis will also need to focus on singing *the liturgy* itself, as distinct from singing hymns during the liturgy, some of which seem far removed from commemorating the life, death and resurrection of Jesus.

---

presence of Christ in the Sacrament. Kneeling for adoration of the Blessed Sacrament is indeed 'laudable'. But the Eucharistic celebration means more than that. A liturgical catechesis based on the *meaning* of the Eucharistic Prayer will focus on what it means to be a redeemed people, raised up with Christ and in union with him come to the Father. As St Augustine says, to 'pray standing . . . is the image of the resurrection' (Letter 55 to Januarius, 15:28). The Council of Nicea (325 AD) made *standing* mandatory for the Lord's day and the fifty days of Eastertide (see J Leonard and N Mitchell, *The Postures of the Assembly during the Eucharistic Prayer* [Liturgy Training Publications, 1994], 23–26). This tradition is echoed in Eucharistic Prayer II. (Even though it has been lost in the new English translation, it is still there in the Latin.)

(vi) Translations

> The purpose of liturgical translations is to proclaim the message of salvation to believers and to express the prayer of the Church . . . To achieve this end, it is not sufficient that a liturgical translation merely reproduce the expressions and ideas of the original text. Rather it must faithfully communicate to a given people, and in their own language, that which the Church by means of this given text originally intended to communicate to another people in another time. The translator must always keep in mind that the 'unit of meaning' is not the individual word but the whole passage. (Instruction *Comme le prevoit*, January 1969, pars 6, 12)

That Instruction guided the first vernacular translations after the Second Vatican Council. The English translation took seriously the need for intelligibility and communication. After all, the Council had said 'In the restoration and promotion of the sacred liturgy, full and active participation by all people is the aim to be considered *before all else*', and for the sake of enabling that kind of participation it wanted the texts and rites to be 'distinguished by simplicity' and 'able to be understood with ease':

> Texts and rites should be drawn up so that they express more clearly the holy things which they signify. Christian people, as far as possible, should be able to understand them with ease and to take part in them fully, actively, and as it befits a community (*SC* 21; see also 31).

The 2002 Instruction, *Liturgiam Authenticam*, however, which juridically superseded the 1969 Instruction, is more concerned with the individual words of the original text, and is ambiguous about the need for the texts to be easy to understand.[6] Consequently, the translations in the new (3rd edition) of the Missal tend to be rigorously literal. They better reflect the nuances of the Latin originals and their biblical allusions. This adds a richness beyond what we have been used to. Their main weakness, however, is that the syntax is often still in Latin even though the vocabulary is in

6. In two adjacent sentences it says:
   It should be borne in mind that a literal translation of terms which may initially sound odd in a vernacular language may for this very reason provoke inquisitiveness in the hearer and provide an occasion for catechesis (43).
   In order for a translation to be more easily proclaimed, it is necessary that any expression be avoided which is confusing or ambiguous when heard, such that the hearer would fail to grasp its meaning (44).

English; for example, long sentences with multiple relative clauses. In a culture of sound-bites and shorter attention spans, many will find these prayers difficult to follow. Proclaiming them prayerfully and intelligibly will require serious preparation ahead of every celebration.

There are two moments in the process of enabling the Church's prayer to become the prayer of the congregation. First there is the faithful translation of the texts, making their meaning available on the pages of the liturgical books. Those translations then have to be lifted off the pages and given voice. The work done by translators does not dispense with the role of presiding. Presiders would be failing in their ministry if they merely parroted the written text regardless of the different circumstances and levels of understanding of the congregation. The choices authorised by the liturgical books themselves are

> so that the celebration may be adapted in an intelligent manner to the church building, or to the group of faithful who are present, or to particular pastoral circumstances in such a way that the universal sacred rite is truly accommodated to human understanding (*Consilium for Implementing the Constitution on the Liturgy*, 1965, Notitiae, 254).

The *General Instruction of the Roman Missal*, 2003 insists, rightly, that 'language should be used that is adapted to the faithful of the region . . . ', 392. Where the translation fails to do this, responsibility falls back on those who are ministers of the word. They are not changing what is *given* in the Church's liturgy by making accommodations that better enable people to *enter into* what is given. Some accommodations are a matter of common sense and courtesy.

Presiding and other ministers must use language that enables all to know they truly *belong* and feel *included*. The Council made 'full and active participation by all . . . the aim to be considered above all else' (*SC* 14). Nothing takes precedence over that.

Hopefully, one day a leader with the vision and courage of the apostle to the gentiles will allow a form of the Roman rite to be *written in English*. The Anglican Prayer Book is testimony to how the beauty, power and poetry of the English language can express in a simple, direct and dignified way what no mere translation from Latin can do. Perhaps this will come to us through the Anglican Communion itself. The Apostolic Constitution (2009) establishing Ordinariates for groups of Anglicans entering full communion with the Catholic Church aims 'to maintain the liturgical, spiritual and pastoral traditions of the Anglican Communion within the Catholic Church as a precious gift nourishing the faith of members of the Ordinariates and as a treasure to be shared' (n III). (The Ordinariates are not new Rites, though we do have more than one form of the Roman Rite.)

(vii) Liturgical Norms

Renewal must also affect the way we think of Church laws and norms. When commissioning a new Code of Canon Law, Pope Paul VI taught that we need not only new formulations of the Church's laws, but a 'new way of thinking' (*novus mentis habitus*) about Church laws.

This, too, is a matter of recovering our Catholic tradition. In that tradition, the law is important because it points us in the direction of what is right. But more is involved than just the letter of the law (as Jesus had to remind the scribes and pharisees many times). The *purpose* intended by the law is the point. Nor does the law make our moral decisions for us. Personal judgments are still required because circumstances and intentions also come into responsible moral decision-making.

The same is true of liturgical norms. In fact, these allow for more flexibility than does canon law.

> The sharp distinction between canon law and liturgical norms follows from the natural difference between the external structures of the Church and its intimate life of worship. Each needs to be ordered and regulated but in different ways. The main purpose of the canons is to build, to support, and to safeguard the necessary societal structures. The aim of liturgical norms is to help the community to recall God's mighty deeds and to experience his presence through the celebration of the mysteries. In this difference of intent there is an important clue regarding the interpretation of each set of norms.
>
> There should be stability in the external order; hence, exceptions from structural and disciplinary laws should not be easily granted. There should be flexibility in worship according to the spiri-

> tual needs of the people; hence, adaptations should be more easily forthcoming (*The Code of Canon Law, A Text and Commentary*, edited by James Coriden [Paulist Press, 1985], 26).

Occasionally, the Congregation for Divine Worship and Sacraments issues 'Instructions'. These are not intended to add any further obligation to existing laws, nor take away from what existing laws allow. They merely apply the law (see c 34). In order to comply with a liturgical Instruction faithfully, we need to ask ourselves: what are the values that this Instruction intends to safeguard? When we know that, we more easily discern how, and how far, the Instruction applies in given situations. For example, norms and modifications more recently put in place by the Holy See can be seen as having two main *purposes*: they are intended

i. to enhance our sense of the sacred. When that is their purpose, the norms themselves are *relative* to that purpose; therefore each is more important or less important depending on how necessary it is for safeguarding our sense of the sacred. (The various rubrics regarding the distribution of Holy Communion come under this description);
ii. to emphasise the difference between the *priesthood* of the priest and the *priestliness* of all the baptised. Again, the importance of each norm depends on how necessary it is for obviating any confusion regarding this difference.

To keep a proper perspective it helps to remember that Instructions are often written to correct situations that do not necessarily exist everywhere. This does not mean they can be disregarded. (Some of St Paul's best writing was done when he was addressing particular situations that needed to be corrected.) It does, nevertheless, highlight the need for good pastoral judgements to be made at local level.[7]

7. In an interview, Feb 2007, the Secretary of the Congregation for Divine Worship and Sacraments claimed that the Church's liturgical reform had been more negative than positive, that the churches have become empty, and that 'liturgical free-wheeling has become the order of the day'. It seemed appropriate to point out to him (letter 25 March 2007), that such exaggerations reinforce the fears of those who have begun to think the Council might have been a mistake; that thanks to the Second Vatican Council, the Catholic people now participate more consciously in the prayers of the Mass itself and hear the word of God more fully and more clearly from the Lectionaries. It was also suggested to him that it would be nice if he and the Cardinal Prefect had something *affirming* to say of those priests who conscientiously and responsibly lead

The dispositions of mind and heart that we need for liturgical renewal to unfold according to *the mind of the Church* are a genuine love for the Church and its liturgy, thinking and feeling with the Church—*sentire cum ecclesia* —and the deepening of our personal prayer life. With these dispositions we more easily recognise the meaning of liturgical norms.

(viii) 'Liturgy of the World'

The phrase is Karl Rahner's. It serves as a corrective to any inward-looking, satisfaction-seeking, individualistic or polished-performance misconceptions of liturgy. Searle comments as follows:

> The liturgy of Christ's death and resurrection is the culmination of the whole dramatic unfolding of living and dying, of warring and loving, of joy and sin and suffering and growth that makes up human history . . .
>
> At the Church's liturgy we have the opportunity to identify with that whole unimaginable history of birth and death, of suffering and joy, which Christ took upon himself and redeemed when he became one of us (*Called to Participate*, 79).

Another way of putting it is:

> I think of the tragedy of hunger which plagues hundreds of millions of human beings, the diseases which afflict developing countries, the loneliness of the elderly, the hardships faced by the unemployed, the struggles of immigrants . . . We cannot delude ourselves: by our mutual love, and in particular, by our concern for those in need we will be recognised as true followers of Christ (cf John 13:35; Matt 25:31–46). This will be the criterion by which the authenticity of our Eucharistic celebrations is judged. (Pope John Paul II, Apostolic Letter for the Year of the Eucharist, *Mane Nobiscum Domine*, 2004, (*MND*) 28) Emphasis added.

---

the liturgy according to the Order of the Mass approved by Pope Paul VI.

Letter Fifteen

Homilies

Dear homilists,

Every priest knows that in ministering to others he is being ministered to. We quickly discover that it is the faith and hopes, struggles, sacrifices, goodness and love of the people that inspire our faith, our desire to serve, and our ability to persevere. The support that priests and people receive from each other is out of proportion to the merits of either; it has the Holy Spirit as its source.

Yet this relationship, on which so much else hangs, is sometimes under strain from inadequate preaching. Does anything cause more concern for parents of adolescents, more frustration and even alienation, than poor preaching? Even apart from issues of presentation, I think we need to review the nature and purpose of homilies.

Moralistic preaching can weigh people down with a feeling of failure and guilt because the 'law' on its own does not empower us for what it demands of us. Homilies have a different dynamic. While sermons are mainly about *what we should do*, homilies point to *what God is doing*. It is preceded by the three scripture readings which form a backdrop—a mosaic—in which we learn to see how God has been present in history; in people's lives; how God has spoken 'at various times and in various ways . . . to our ancestors' (cf Heb 1:1). We become familiar with God's style. Then the homily makes connections, by helping us to see how God has been just as truly present in our own lives.

The discovery of God's marvellous, surprising, unmerited love generates our desire to love and to live gratefully in return. It liberates and empowers us for even more than the law asks of us. Notice what happened to Zacchaeus (Lk 19:1–10): he presumed that Jesus never even knew him, and then heard himself being called by his name, and honoured by Jesus' visit to his place. This empowered him to turn his life around. The surprise and experience of God's love for him gave him new freedom, and the *desire* to do what was right.

The prophet Jeremiah claimed he had been 'seduced' by God's love. He did not want the mission God was giving him; in fact, he hated it. But he could not resist the love that he knew had always looked after him. That is how it works when we realise how much we are loved. It is hard to imagine the Samaritan woman whom Jesus met at Jacob's well, or Mary Magdalen, or the apostle Peter, or the woman accused of committing adultery, or the blind and lame that Jesus met along the road, ever being content with merely fulfilling their minimum obligations. The hope and joy that come with the discovery of God's love are uncrippling!

The point here is *not* that these people are being proposed as good examples for us to follow; (that would not rise above the level of *what we should do*); the point is *what God is doing*, and what happens to people when their eyes are opened to that.[1]

This does not mean that the scripture readings are reducible to mere information about how we might find God in our lives. Rather, God is addressing us personally in the scripture readings, helping us to see the meaning of our lives within the unfolding script of 'salvation history'. We find we are included.[2]

But God's word does not work mechanically; it is not magic. It is only 'good news' because it confirms something that deep down we already needed to know, or suspected might be so. People need to be in touch with those yearnings God has placed in human nature, that are hints of our being made for something more. The word is Good News when it comes to us as *assurance* that our deepest longings (for life, love, peace, freedom,

1. The lives of saints (including the ones we know) can work on us in the same way. And genuine eulogies also point to how God was present in another ordinary life.
2. Religious education is different again; it is *about* God and the Christian life, and belongs to a time and place outside the liturgy. Catechesis, however, does have a place within homilies because it fosters personal adherence to Christ.

belonging . . .) are destined to be fulfilled. If it does not 'connect' with what deeply matters to us, then we hear but don't see the point.

> The failure of conventional religion is that it does not evoke the spiritual roots of our journeying. It assumes that everyone can hear the scriptures 'neat', or enter the wave-length of the liturgy without difficulty. Instead many people are nowhere near the threshold of such readiness. They are untouched by ceremonies that were forged for another culture. They are in need of a more sensitive initiation into their own spiritual drama. (Michael Paul Gallagher, *Dive Deeper*, [London: DLT, 2002], 9).[3]

We have long since been familiar with James Fowler's *Stages of Faith*, but what kind of opportunities do we create for people to talk about their feelings of doubt and disenchantment that are necessarily part of transitioning from one stage to another? What Gallagher calls their 'sensitive initiation into their own spiritual drama' properly belongs to all the times and places of spiritual direction, pastoral counselling and catechesis. But in the homely manner that is proper to a homily (the Greek word *homilein* means 'to converse'), the homilist has a role to play in interpreting those longings and experiences of pre-religious awareness, such as

- when something wonderful in nature leaves us feeling we are part of something much bigger than our own lifetime. Or when the sudden feeling that even the good things of life (a good marriage, a successful business, good friends, good health, etc) still leave an empty gap somewhere inside us. Our own deep self tells us that there's something more than all this;
- or when someone we love has died, and suddenly everything around us appears in a different light; the things that seemed so important don't seem quite so important now, and the things that seemed remote, like heaven, suddenly seem so real;
- or when some sight or sound or scent triggers some fond memory and we know we are still linked to people and places of our past. There's a

3. A pastor of the Apostolic Church once told me that many of his congregation were Catholics. They too, had felt 'untouched by ceremonies that were forged for another culture' and found his services more congenial. He was happy to meet their needs, but saw this as part of their journey; he told me he always encourages Catholics and Anglicans eventually to return to their true home. His next remark was unforgettable: 'we are happy to be the doormat over which they walk on their way home'.

feeling that they are still part of us, and that one day all good things will come together again;

- or when we are listening to the kind of music that makes us want to be still and quiet because it seems to be drawing us towards something. Or, when in some quiet space on our own, we just experience the mystery or our own self, unique in all the universe. So Why?
- or when in some life-giving experience we know intuitively that life is what we were made for. Unself-conscious expressions of love, of delight and of play are all sacramental—human embodiments of God's own delight in creation. Nothing is more life-giving that the experience of love, which draws us beyond ourselves 'to join not just a duet of intimacy but a symphony of full life' (Gallagher, *ibid*, 24);
- even the experiences that leave us without answers such as failures from within ourselves or the mystery of someone else's suffering can lead us beyond the need for answers to a deeper peace that mere answers would not have given us. God's healing presence quietly assures us that in the end 'all will be well, and all manner of things will be well' (Julian of Norwich).

All these special moments are like occasional springs of water for the journey through the desert of 'ordinary' life. Once assured that God really is 'with us', then we can know God's companionship in the 'ordinary' little events of life as well.

'God with us' comes into special focus in the person of Jesus. His life, death and resurrection reveal the meaning of the experiences we have been describing. For this, the Church needs a 'language' that helps to make sense of people's religious experiences. Much of the needed language, of course, will be that of symbol and ritual, and of experiences that lead to wonder and hope, healing and compassion, and it will be the fruit of contemplation.

A contemplative is one who 'sees' God in the events of salvation history—past and present (see Epilogue). The contemplative homilist invites people to see what he sees. There is nothing 'soft' about this approach to preaching. It is challenging in the way that St Paul challenged Christians: having alerted them to their true dignity as greatly loved by God, he expected them to live in a way that corresponded to that great dignity.

We also need to be one with the people we speak to: 'We must put ourselves in their shoes, hear with their ears, smart with their wounds, feel with their skin' (T Radcliffe OP, *Why Go to Church?* [London: Continuum, 2008], 57).

Finally, we need to provide more opportunities for lay men and women to share their reflections on the scriptures. There is a ministry of the word that belongs to ordained ministry (c 767/1). But there are also situations that make it 'necessary in certain circumstances or useful in particular cases' for lay persons to 'preach in a church' (c 766) and 'exercise the ministry of the word' (c 230/3). This would not ordinarily replace the homily, but sometimes this can be appropriate, especially at Masses for children (cf Directory for Children's Masses, 1973, 24), and when people's right to hear the word of God would not otherwise be properly provided for.

Letter Sixteen

Christian Unity—Having a Heart for it

Dear Bill & Gillian,

You were raised Catholic and Anglican respectively and in the early years of your marriage you worshiped in both your churches each Sunday. This could not have been easy for you especially when the children were young, and more so because of your cerebral palsy, Bill. Your commitment to God and to each other suggests that perhaps it is to couples in inter-church marriages that we need to turn to give the work for Christian unity a needed boost. The need for unity would be felt more keenly by people like you.

The 'ecumenical movement' started among other Christians. Within the Catholic Church many who longed for unity were lay people. But now all Christians are indebted to Popes John XXIII, Paul VI, John Paul II and Benedict XVI for the giant steps that have been taken by the See of Peter.

For Catholics, working for Christian unity is actually a requirement of being a Catholic. Pope John Paul II put it this way:

> Ecumenism, the work of promoting Christian unity, is not just a sort of 'appendix' which is added to the Church's traditional activities. It is an organic part of her life and work and must pervade all that she is and does. (Encyclical Letter On Commitment to Ecumenism *Ut Unum Sint*, 1995 (*UUS*) 20;

including, therefore, her renewal.

The most serious obstacle to Christian unity is people's willingness to look no further than co-existence and co-operation—as if what divides us doesn't really matter. The Church's mission is to proclaim what God is doing in the world—reconciling all things in Christ. We are called to be ambassadors of that reconciliation (2 Cor 5:17–20). Can we expect to be credible if we have opted to live with disunity on questions affecting the very nature of discipleship? Do we not impair the credibility of Jesus' own mission (cf Jn 17:21)?

It is not enough to say that the fullness of unity belongs to the eschaton. Of course it does. But the Church's mission is to be a sign, here and now, of that eschaton—a sign of the reconciliation and the unity of all things in Christ. Similarly, it is meaningless to relegate unity to the realm of the invisible. The Church's mission is to *make visible* what God is doing in Christ. And so our unity needs to be *visible* in what we actually believe and profess to do.

The danger for Roman Catholics is that, because we believe we have preserved doctrine, sacraments and ministries intact, we can easily assume that ecumenism is not our problem. The danger for other Christians is that it is difficult to visualise—and therefore easy to underestimate—how far even the Roman Catholic Church can be re-imagined, re-shaped and re-expressed just in the way its beliefs are formulated, its sacraments celebrated, and its ministries carried out. The *content* of our faith is one thing; how we say it, profess it, live it, nurture it and minister to it is another. It is the *how* that projects our image, and creates our perceptions of one another. Pope John XXIII did not change the Catholic Church's teaching concerning the ministry of the Pope. Yet the minds and hearts of many were changed. Perceptions were changed by *how* his ministry was carried out.

In his Encyclical UUS, Pope John Paul II speaks of 'the necessary and sufficient visible unity', and he invokes the teaching of the Council of Jerusalem (Acts 15:28) that we must 'not impose any burden beyond that which is strictly necessary' (78).

So how much visible unity is 'necessary and sufficient?' It is hardly surprising that the Church's teaching on a 'hierarchy of truths' is to be found in its Decree on Ecumenism (*Unitatis Redintegratio*, 1964 (*UR*)11. Some truths of our faith are more central to the mystery of Christ than are others. This does not mean the others are less true, or that they do not matter. It means that they are *less central* to the core of Christian revelation.

The more central truths need to become the basis for a sufficient degree of organic unity *even before* it is possible to reach unity around the less central truths of our faith.

In fact, this needs to happen *so that* we can reach further agreement, because how Christians—of whatever denomination—come to think of their faith and express it in words depends on how they have first *experienced* it. The experience takes place within the tradition one belongs to. So, for example, what Catholics believe concerning Mary's Immaculate Conception and Assumption, was eventually able to be expressed as *doctrines* of the Catholic faith because Catholics had already *experienced* these beliefs as part of their Catholic lives and devotion. Denominations that have not had the same experience of the Christian faith could not come to the same perceptions and expressions of it. A fuller sharing of the experience of Christian faith is necessary *so that* there can eventually be a more united profession of it. (See Letter 17.)

Strikingly, in his Encyclical, Pope John Paul II acknowledged that Christians need to '*seek together* the forms' in which his ministry might be more easily recognised by all (cf *UUS* 95). Shared seeking leads to shared conclusions.

There is an interplay between the doctrines of faith in that each throws light on the others and helps to illustrate their meaning. Both the renewal of the Church, and its attractiveness to others, will depend on us living *all* the truths of our faith, but with greater devotion to those that are more central.

The movement to fuller unity involves being attracted by the faith that we see *in each other*. Those of us who have been involved in ecumenical dialogues and inter-church activities know that something more happens when we get down to praying together. That is when we more clearly recognise that others' faith in Christ and love for Christ are as real as our own, or as we would like ours to be. And so we experience more keenly the futility and the pain of being divided.

This pain, in turn, can deepen our resolve to pray and work for overcoming our divisions. That resolve will be the weaker if we have not first experienced the pain of being divided, and we do not experience that pain until we are next to each other in prayer.

So much the better if this happens where the other is most 'at home' in prayer. We experience each other's faith within the context of the tradition, or denomination, that has nurtured it. Specially devised ecumenical services do not represent any one tradition in particular, and so cannot reveal to us where the others' faith has found its nurture.

Of course, problems of reciprocity arise if it is the Mass we think of for this shared experience. But that is not our only option. We can pray together in our homes!

And what would happen if as Catholics we restored our own tradition of coming together for the Church's Evening Prayer on Sunday evenings? This is a liturgy of the Church that others can fully participate in. How far are we prepared to go for the sake of being with one another in prayer?

This 'spiritual' ecumenism is something each one of us can be part of. It provides the undergirding experience that gives warmth, focus and direction to ecumenical dialogue. As Pope John Paul II puts it: 'fellowship in prayer leads people to look at the Church and Christianity in a new way' (*UUS* 23).

Ultimately, the work of promoting Christian unity is a journey of rediscovering what once belonged to us all. This can sometimes be better expressed in the terms and symbols that we used before we began to define ourselves by how we are different from each other, provided this does not become an exercise in archaism. It is how we express the faith today that needs to be the fruit of Christian unity.

For all of us, the journey is into a deeper relationship with Christ. In converging on him, we come closer to each other.

In an interview published under the title: *Crossing the Threshold of Hope* (Random House, Jonathan Cape, London, 1994) Pope John Paul II was asked: why did the Holy Spirit permit all these divisions to occur? He gave the only answer that could be given: God could only allow the divisions to happen because of some greater good that will eventually result from them. He dared to ask:

> Could it not be that these divisions have also been a path continually leading the Church to discover the untold wealth contained in Christ's Gospel and in the redemption . . . ?
>
> Perhaps all this wealth would not have come to light otherwise . . . (153).

With the same kind of courage, it is time to ask ourselves: what might not have come to light so easily if the Church had not become divided? Might the continuing reluctance of other Christians to be organically united with us have anything to do with the questions raised in Letter 11 that we seem so reluctant to address? What openings to renewal does God intend to come to us through the journey to full unity?

Letter Seventeen

Christian Unity—Making Spaces for it

Dear Cardinal Prefect,

I write in the spirit of the collegial co-responsibility your predecessor, Cardinal E Cassidy, clearly had in mind when he told the Synod of Bishops in 1991:

> We in the Pontifical Council for Promoting Christian Unity have been given the task of working for the unity of Christians; but the task is one that the Second Vatican Council entrusted to all the bishops and local churches (*CIC* 755).
>
> We look to you in this Synod to speak to us and illumine us on this aspect of evangelisation . . . Not enough has been done as yet in general in the Catholic Church to put into practice the ecumenical principles set forth in the Council documents, and particularly to discern their pastoral consequences (Address to Special Assembly for Europe).

The Cardinal was inviting bishops to do more than defer to the competence of the Holy See, and reminding us that this work had been 'entrusted to all the bishops and local churches'.

No one would doubt that the international theological dialogues have played, and continue to play, an essential role in this ongoing work. But we should not expect more of theological dialogue than it is capable of achieving. Full communion will indeed involve a common profession of faith, and therefore genuine agreement on the meaning of what we profess. But how we reach that agreement involves more than theological dialogue. It requires a greater *shared experience of the faith.* The connection between how the faith is experienced and how it is conceptualised and articulated deserves greater attention.

Many years ago, it was claimed that the experience of the Third World Conference of Faith and Order (Lund 1952) and the subsequent work of the Theological Commission (1954) showed that no progress could be made simply by comparing doctrinal positions. Such an approach starts from a given disunity. The need was felt to start from the God-given unity already possessed and 'to draw the consequences of this existing unity for the actual life of the Church and for the togetherness of the denominations'. (Marron, V, 'The Ecumenical Development of Theology', in *Doctrinal Development and Christian Unity*, edited by Nicholas Lash [London: Sheed &Ward, 1967], 76).

In a general sense, we accept easily enough that 'the less one has participated in the Christian religious experience, the less one is capable of appreciating the doctrines that articulate the meaning of that experience' (Chirico, P, 'Religious Experience and Development of Dogma', in *The American Benedictine Review*, Volume 23, Number 1 1972: 70). But we are strangely slow to acknowledge the ecumenical implications of this important fact. The context in which the different Christian denominations perceive and formulate the meaning of their faith results from the different historical, cultural, social and theological environments in which they live their faith. And the less one has participated in their experience of the faith, the less one is able to appreciate what they mean.

There is evidence for this from an even older ecumenical experience. At the Council of Florence (1438–42) which had been called to heal the schism of the East and the West, significant doctrinal agreement was reached. But the agreement meant little to those who had not participated in the experience out of which the agreed formulations emerged. And so nothing came of it. (cf Macha, J, *Ecclesiastical Unification: A Theoretical Framework together with Case Studies from the History of Latin-Byzantine Relations* [Rome: Pontifical Institutum Orientalium Studiorum, 1974], 122.)

ARCIC I had already reached the conclusion that 'some difficulties will not be wholly resolved until a practical initiative has been taken and our two churches have lived together more visibly in one koinonia.' (*Authority in the Church II*, Statement, n 33.)

Whatever the shape of such 'living together more visibly' may or may not be, it is at least certain that doctrinal differences cannot be resolved on the basis of intellectual comparisons of formulated teaching.

> The human mind never verifies this agreement (between the convictions of different people) simply by establishing the identical nature of the conceptual content. Real community, identical *utterances* (as opposed to purely abstract thinking), and common concrete action are necessary elements in verifying the sameness of many people's convictions.
>
> . . . Common concrete activity (in the broadest sense) is not only the result of a shared conviction: it is also the way in which we fashion this common conviction and come to take cognisance of it . . . Indeed we will find a oneness that can never be provided by concepts alone. (Rahner, K, 'Pluralism in Theology & the Unity of the Church's Profession of Faith', in *Concilium*, Volume 6, Number 5 1969: 57.)

Rahner had shown in several of his writings that there is an unavoidable gap between the contents of individuals' own personal, explicit faith, and the full contents of the Church's faith. Notwithstanding this 'gap', all the truths of faith are encompassed by the act of faith. This is also the teaching of St Thomas (*Summa Theologiae,* Pars 11, Quaestio 1, art ad 2 am). As the believer's faith develops, it gradually assimilates and situates the various 'objects of faith'. The same is true for particular groups within the Church, and at particular epochs in the Church's history.[1]

This is why the Church does not need to require explicit faith in *all* the Church's doctrines as a precondition for participation in the Church's life. The obvious example is the Church's practice in regard to the Confirmation and first Holy Communion of children. But nor is this a mere

1. (See Rahner, What is Heresy? *Theological Investigations,* Volume 5, chapter 19: 'On the Theology of the Ecumenical Discussion', in *Theological Investigations*, Volume 11, chapter 12; 'Heresies in the Church Today?', in *Theological Investigations*, Volume 12, chapter 7; 'The Faith of the Christian and The Doctrine of the Church', in *Theological Investigations*, Volume 14, chapter 2.

concession to childhood. In the early Church, the adult catechumen was required to make a confession of faith (the Creed) which was only a summary, and did not even include such an essential doctrine as the Eucharist. (See Schillebeeckx, E, 'Revelation and Theology', *Theological Soundings*, Volume 1, part 1, [London & Sydney: Sheed & Ward, 1967], 231).

The reality of gaps between personal faith and the full doctrine of the Church is implicit in the practice of oikonomia:

> Economy is not an attitude of doctrinal liberalism, for it does not consist of keeping silence on a point of faith, or of reducing necessary belief to a common denominator or dogmas acceptable to all; nor is it a matter of minimising the meaning of doctrine, but of keeping silence for the time being concerning certain aspects or certain logical consequences, for reasons of charity; of not making explicit certain formulations which would unnecessarily hurt the weak from the time they accept to profess the common faith in equivalent terms. (Lanne, E *Les Differences Compatibles avec L'unite Dans La Tradition de L'Eglise Ancienne* (Jusqu'au XII siècle) Istina 1961–62: 246.)

These are the kind of considerations that need to be taken into account when applying the Council's teaching that

> In order to restore communion and unity or preserve them, one must 'impose no burden beyond what is indispensible'. (Acts 15:28). It is the Council's urgent desire that every effort should henceforth be made towards the gradual realisation of this goal in the various organisations and living activities of the Church, especially by prayer and by fraternal dialogue on points of doctrine and the more pressing pastoral problems of our time. (Decree on Ecumenism, n 18).

It is a matter of creating the kind of spaces people need for growing into the truth. There is an echo of this in pope Benedict's reason for lifting the excommunication of the bishops of the Society of St Pius X *before* they were ready to be fully reconciled with the Church. He wanted 'to make space for what is positive and retrievable for the whole'. Later, in his letter to the Catholic bishops (2009), he went on to say: 'I myself saw in the years after 1988 how the return of communities which had been separated from Rome changed their interior attitudes; I saw how returning to the bigger and broader Church enabled them to move beyond one-sided positions . . .'

The Decree on Ecumenism called on us to recognise a hierarchy of importance within the Church's teachings. A satisfying interpretation of this has been given by the International Theological Commission which explains that since the subject (the 'I') of the Creed is the Church, those expressions of faith which are more universal are more expressive of the Church's identity and therefore of its faith. On this basis, scripture takes priority over all subsequent formulations; the ancient Creeds over the Councils; the Councils of Nicea and Chalcedon over all other Councils (because they were concerned with the most central and therefore most universal truths of the Creed); and those dogmatic formulas which more directly relate to the facts of salvation history over those which involve theological reflection on those facts. (Cf Ratzinger, J editor *Pluralismo; unita della fede e pluralismo teologico* [Bologna, Edizioni Dehoniane, 1974], 43–48.)

At the very least, the Second Vatican Council was saying that the truths of our faith, even though they all belong, do not all have the same importance, and that in some way this difference between them has implications for the restoration of Christian unity.

When all is said and done, we acknowledge that the apostolic Church already enjoyed the fullness of Christian revelation even though the first generation of Christians could not have said all that we now say as part of our faith. In other words, such is the 'development of doctrine' that those Christians who live sooner and those who live later (in a vertical line down through history) both possess the fullness of the Christian faith, but differently. What makes the difference is ultimately their different experience of the same faith due to the different historical cultural, spiritual and theological environments in which they live their faith. Have we fully explored the extent to which this might also be true horizontally between contemporary Christians living within their different denominational contexts?

This is not to say that we can ignore or acquiesce in real differences. It is to say that because development in how Christians come to perceive and formulate the meaning of their faith depends on the context in which they live it, they can only come to a more common perception and formulation of doctrines through a greater sharing of Christian life and worship.

> Creeds may be regarded as resulting from the inner exigencies of a lived faith; they should not be forcibly imposed, by external authoritative action, upon peoples not prepared for them by their corporate historical experience . . .
>
> In the last analysis, I suspect there are no adequate extrinsic norms for measuring the validity of confessional statements. They cannot be tested against other biblical or creedal utterances by merely syllogistic logic. The norm must be to some extent existential. It is necessary to enter into the spiritual world of the other church with true empathy, and in this way to assess its declarations in relation to ones sense of the Christian reality. Christian reunion therefore presupposes a certain sharing of religious experience on the part of believers of different denominations. (Dulles, A, 'Dogma as an Ecumenical Problem', in *Theological Studies*, 29, 1968: 412, 415.)

The experience from which doctrinal formulations emerge is, at its deepest level, Christians' experience of, and response to, the person of the risen Christ in the community which is united to him and lives by him. This experience is grasped with only limited understanding, which in turn is conceptualised, articulated and communicated, and may eventually become a formulated expression of the faith of the community. Dogmas are limited formulations of limited understanding, starting from what has been experienced.

Even allowing for that wholeness which the Roman Catholic Church claims for itself, it must still be said that the perception, formulation and teaching of Christian truth suffers by that lack of full communion which, when restored, will enrich us all. This claim is indirectly supported by the distinction J Ratzinger makes between 'real' and 'juridical' ecumenicity, when he explains why the ecumenical councils of the Middle Ages are less important for us than the earlier ones, in spite of the fact that they too were 'ecumenical':

> The relationship between these Councils and the Pope assures them of an ecumenicity 'of right'. But the absence of the Oriental Churches signifies nevertheless an incalculable lack of real ecumenicity, which at the same time limits the importance of their

> role in Christian ecumenism. Only a dialogue which includes all the different traditions could make possible the full ecumenicity of their propositions (*Pluralismo*, 47, 48 and *passim*).

We could well learn another lesson from the Church in earlier times: when faced with dissension, a usual practice was to look beyond what was being said to what was being done (and therefore believed) in the liturgy and life of the dissenting group. In our circumstances, we need to create the conditions which would allow for a kind of transfer from the unity we already experience in the context of prayer and Christian living, to unity in our professions of faith.

An opportunity for this kind of sharing was presented to us with the development of the Common Lectionary. In 1970 several Protestant and Anglican Churches adapted the Catholic lectionary (1969) for their own use. The only point of difference is the Common Lectionary's provision of semi-continuous Old Testament readings for Ordinary time after Pentecost. The willingness of several other Christian denominations to have a Common Lectionary based on the Catholic Lectionary, and the desirability of all Christians hearing the same readings every Sunday from a Common Lectionary is consistent with the 1993 *Directory for Applying Principles and Norms on Ecumenism* which calls for 'common scriptural readings for liturgical use'.

I commented to one of your predecessors that it seemed so wrong that the CDWS could, without consulting the universal episcopate, deprive all of us (Catholics and other Christians) of the benefits of this opportunity. It seems perplexing that the 1993 Directory, which is the Church's *ius vigens* for ecumenism, could be so easily disregarded.[2]

In his post-Synodal Apostolic Exhortation on the Word of God, 2010, Pope Benedict spoke of the ecumenical benefits of 'shared listening to the scriptures' (n 46). There is no need for this to be limited to infrequent special occasions; it could be happening every Sunday. But the initiative would have come from the episcopate.

---

2. In 1994, the Executive Committee of the English Language Liturgical Consultation, which has been responsible for developing the Common Lectionary, visited the CDWS requesting that the Congregation consider granting faculties for a limited use of the Common Lectionary. They never received any formal reply.

Letter Eighteen

Marriage and Family Life

Dear married couples preparing others for marriage,

Good marriages (not just Christian marriages) have a special role to play in keeping alive the vision of life and love as *gifts*.

Secularism has its own logic: if there is no personal God to whom we are accountable for how we live our lives, then our lives are ours to dispose of as we will. But then the logic turns sour. Human life becomes useable, disposable and marketable. It becomes property. From that perspective, it really is hard to see what is wrong with bringing embryos into existence, using them as raw material for other ends, and discarding them.[1]

But secularism's logic prevails, and so we find ourselves within a culture that widely trivialises what is sacred, and then idolises what is trivial!

Within a good marriage, on the other hand, we have our deepest experiences of life as a gift, and of ourselves as trustees, not proprietors. That is because within the experience of marriage and family life, people constantly rediscover that love and life are '*mystery*'—they have an origin beyond ourselves; they come to us as something not owed to us.

No one knows this better than a husband and wife when they experience each other's love as something they cannot account for, as somehow

1. It is tempting to be dismissive of comparisons between this and what the Nazis also did in the name of medical research. But the similarities are real: in both cases the victims have no say; in both cases it is claimed to be for other people's benefit. (But whereas the Nazis had ideological reasons as well, we have commercial reasons as well.) In both cases, it is being simply assumed that the end justifies the means.

surprising, as gift. In this love they 'know' God. Their experience keeps alive the knowledge that love ultimately comes to us from beyond ourselves.

The same is true when they experience the fruit of their love in a new life: it can be an experience of wonder and amazement. In this new life they 'see God'. Their experience keeps alive the knowledge that life really is a reason for wonder, gratitude and joy—because it is a gift.

It is for these same reasons that Catholic sexual ethics, and ethics relating to bio-technology and end of life issues, are a strong affirmation of the mystery and wonder of human life. They identify the boundaries of our *limited dominion* over human life—the exact opposite of the view that it is entirely up to us what we do with human life. *Unlimited* dominion presupposes that human life is not a gift of God.

Catholics can afford to be more proud of the Church's teaching that affirms the mystery and wonder of life.

In all these ways, marriage tells the same story that the Church exists to tell—that human life and human love have their origins in the life and love of God. Keeping this message alive, especially in a secular environment, requires that the home be where people have the experience of being loved unconditionally, of deep bonding between parents and children, of deep reverence for life, true respect for each other, and opportunities to take compassion towards others whose lives are more vulnerable, or who do not experience being greatly loved. The home also needs to be where the family hears all these needs being named in family prayer.

Pope Paul VI reminded us that

> At different moments in the Church's history and also at the Second Vatican Council, the family has well deserved the beautiful name of 'domestic Church' . . .
>
> In a family which is conscious of its mission, all the members evangelise and are evangelised. The parents not only communicate the gospel to their children, but they can themselves receive the same gospel back from their children as deeply lived by them. (Apostolic Letter on Evangelisation, n 71)

In a home environment of living faith children experience a sense of the mystery and wonder of life, without which there can be no deep respect for life, no sense of it being a gift, and no reason for living gratefully, humbly and justly.

They learn to echo the kind of prayers people prayed when they met Jesus of Nazareth. Even though some of those prayers presuppose adult experience, they are prayers we *grow into* if we already know them. They are the kind of prayers that carry a sense of how Jesus responded, and still responds, to those who turn to him.

Parents who want to share the greatest gift they can with their children will want their children's earliest and most lasting memories to be something they can come back to, even if for a while they follow wrong paths. Those memories will include how they were taken to visit needy and lonely people.

From earliest years they will hear the stories of men and women of great faith, and see symbols that 'speak' to them about life being bigger than their immediate horizons. They belong to the communion of saints. Never underestimate the power of a good quality holy picture hanging silently above a child's bed where it is contemplated at that precious time when the child opens its eyes on the world at the beginning of each day, or closes them for the night.

Children who learn to hold a crucifix in their hands, look closely at the one on it, remember who he is and why he was there, can eventually say in the words of St Paul: 'you loved me and gave yourself for me' (Gal 2:20). In this way they come to know their life is worthwhile forever, no matter what happens.

They will learn to expect the imperfections of a human Church, and the holiness of a Church that is nevertheless the body of Christ. In that Church they will find the inspiration to be different in a world where so many live without hope, purpose or joy.

In my letter to Theophilus (Letter 1), I echoed the Archbishop of Canterbury's claim that the Church is meant to be 'a living model of renewed social relationships based on renewed relationship with God'. It is especially the vocation of Christian spouses and families to bring this about.

They do this by loving as God loves. On the cross, Jesus showed us what God's love is like: faithful, forgiving, life-giving, unconditional and until death. Ultimately, only this kind of love can transform relationships. That is the kind of love Christian spouses commit themselves to, especially when they take their vows before the altar which, in the Christian tradition, symbolises Jesus' complete, self-giving love on the Cross.

They will be empowered to love as God loves because it will be God's love in them! God's love comes to husband and wife *in their human love for each other*! That is what it means to say Christian marriage is a sacrament.

The support most needed for marriage and family life is that which comes through the 'apostolate of like to like'—couples accompanying couples; families accompanying families.

Letter Nineteen

The Pastoral Care of Separated/Remarried Spouses

Dear Pastors and Lay Pastoral Assistants

It is part of our calling to 'rejoice with those who rejoice and be sad with those in sorrow' (Rom 12:15). There is plenty of scope for both in our work with families and especially with those who have experienced broken marriages.

By now, unfortunately, many of those who have suffered broken marriages, and especially if they have entered new relationships, have made up their minds that there is nothing the Church can do for them; they feel excluded, and see no point in being involved with the Church. Even if they are wrong in this, that is their perception. After all, oversimplified preaching and teaching in the past created the impression that divorce *excluded* them.

> . . . testimony from a number of priests who work in programmes with alienated Catholics indicates that the single biggest reason people cease active participation in the Church is that they have found themselves in irregular marital situations and feel unwanted and rejected by the Church. Exclusion from the Eucharist is the most commonly cited expression of how the Church manifests its non-acceptance of the divorced and remarried (Kenneth R Himes, OFM and James A Coriden, 'Pastoral Care of the Divorced and Remarried', in *Theological Studies*, March 1996: 118).

Those who feel distanced from the Church stand to lose much, and for that reason so does the Church. Our ministry to them and the renewal of the Church belong together.

I offer these reflections in support of your efforts to be ambassadors of reconciliation (see 2 Cor 5:17–20) and bearers of hope. First (part 1) some general comments, and then (part 2) pastoral practices and future possibilities.

Part 1—General Comments

In a society that accepts divorce and remarriage as perfectly normal, the Church has no option but to be counter-cultural—witnessing to the indissolubility of marriage.

> To bear witness to the inestimable value of the indissolubility and fidelity of marriage is one of the most precious and most urgent tasks of Christian couples in our time . . . I praise and encourage those numerous couples who . . . perform the role committed to them of being in the world a 'sign'—a small and precious sign . . . of the unfailing fidelity with which God and Jesus Christ love each and every human being. It is also proper to recognise the value of the witness of those spouses who, even when abandoned by their partner, with the strength of faith and of Christian hope have not entered a new union: these spouses too give an authentic witness to fidelity, of which the world today has a great need. For this reason they must be encouraged and helped by the pastors and faithful of the Church. (Pope John Paul II, Post Synodal Exhortation on the Christian Family in the Modern World, *Familiaris Consortio*, 1981, (*FC*) 20)

The scriptures are clear that Jesus revoked the allowance Moses had made for divorce and remarriage, intending to restore marriage to 'how it was in the beginning' (which, rather than an historical assertion, just means 'how God intended it') (cf Mk 10:2–12; Matt 19:3–9; 1 Cor 7:10, 11).

Yet down the centuries, dating back to the apostle Paul, the Church has claimed authority to dissolve non-sacramental marriages in given circumstances; (cf 1 Cor 7:12–16). So, upholding the indissolubility of marriage and exercising compassion in this way, *both* belong to the Catholic tradition.

Compassion and the reality of human failure also lie behind the Church's practice of examining whether some marriages were valid in the first place, and if not, declaring them null.[1] Nor does the Church's pastoral concern finish there: it continues even when a Catholic enters a second, non-canonical marriage. These Catholics, too, are full members of the Church; many of them seek help at the level of conscience, and some of them still long to receive the sacraments of Penance and Holy Communion.

In recent decades, numerous theological and canonical writings have explored how we might do more for couples who have experienced broken marriages, including those who have entered a second but invalid marriage. A Pastoral Letter written in 1993 by three German bishops, including the President and Vice-President of the German Bishops' Conference and Bishop (now Cardinal) Kasper, which was followed by a Letter from the Congregation for the Doctrine of the Faith to all bishops (1994), and then a reply by the three German bishops, intensified the debate across the world. The issue is not the indissolubility of marriage; it is how to combine this teaching with the need for compassion given the reality of human failure. The challenge, in my view, is not how to hold in tension two seemingly opposite concerns, but how to truly *integrate* both concerns as essential components of the Catholic tradition and therefore not contradictory. That is the perspective from which this letter is being written. The exercise is not academic. It is about people's lives and consciences.

Our approach to how we might further help these Catholics needs to be governed by our commitment to the full ideal of Christian marriage and family life. Those we are trying to help ultimately do not want us to give them, or others, a diminished gospel.

Nor can we forget that right across the spectrum of life, Christian faith does not allow us to indulge in the assumption that there has to be a happy solution—within the horizons of our present life—to every situation. The gospel gives no such assurance, and on the contrary clearly forewarns that faithfulness to following Christ can cost us our lives. It can sometimes be necessary to forgo the exercise of our own rights if others could be led astray by what they see (for example, 1 Cor 8: 9–12).

1. That is, valid as the Church understands marriage; and null in the eyes of the Church.

When all is said and done, however,

> Various reasons can unfortunately lead to the often irreparable break-down of valid marriages. These include mutual lack of understanding, and the inability to enter into inter-personal relationships. Obviously, separation must be considered as a last resort, after all other reasonable attempts at reconciliation have proved vain (John Paul II, *FC* 83).

Our focus should not be narrowed down to restoring them to the sacraments, and much less should we compromise truth and justice in order to do that. Our primary aim should be to help them grow in the life of faith, hope and love, which is still possible even when receiving the sacraments is not. But nor should we too easily presume that sacramental practice is not possible.

Part 2—Pastoral Practices and Future Possibilities

Speaking of those who are separated, though not divorced, Pope John Paul II says:

> Loneliness and other difficulties are often the lot of separated spouses, especially when they are the innocent parties. The ecclesial community must support such people more than ever. It must given them much respect, solidarity, understanding and practical help, so that they can preserve their fidelity even in their difficult situation; and it must help them to cultivate the need to forgive which is inherent in Christian love, and to be ready perhaps to return to their former married life (*FC* 83).

Then speaking of those who are divorced and remarried, the pope calls on us to ensure they feel included in the life of the Church:

> I earnestly call upon pastors and the whole community of the faithful to help the divorced, and with solicitous care to make sure that they do not consider themselves as separated from the Church, for as baptised persons they can, and indeed must, share in her life. They should be encouraged to listen to the word of God, to attend the sacrifice of the Mass, to persevere in prayer, to contribute to works of charity and to community efforts in favour of justice, to bring up their children in the Christian faith, to cultivate the spirit

> and practice of penance, and thus implore, day by day, God's grace. Let the Church pray for them, encourage them and show herself a merciful mother, and thus sustain them in faith and in hope (*FC* 84).

At the same time, he reiterates the Church's practice

> . . . of not admitting to Eucharistic communion divorced persons who have remarried . . .
>
> Reconciliation in the Sacrament of Penance which would open the way to the Eucharist, can only be granted to those who, repenting of having broken the sign of the Covenant and of fidelity to Christ, are sincerely ready to undertake a way of life that is no longer in contradiction to the indissolubility of marriage. This means, in practice, that when, for serious reasons such as for example the children's' upbringing, a man and a woman cannot satisfy the obligations to separate, they take on themselves the duty to live in complete continence, that is by abstinence from the acts proper to married couples (*FC* 84).

This is as we should expect to find the general teaching of the Church. It needs to be noted that papal teachings, General Instructions and Catechisms normally focus on general principles and norms, consciously leaving it to moral theology to deal with the subjective factors that necessarily belong to every concrete situation. The need for the Church to function at *both* these levels derives from the fact that the formulation of laws and the processes of law simply cannot adequately cover every human circumstance.[2] Precisely because of this inbuilt inadequacy, applying the law according to its letter can sometimes result in very serious and even unjust consequences for individuals. It properly belongs to moral theology, often in the context of the internal forum, to guide consciences in these situations.

This long-standing practice of the Church was acknowledged by the Congregation for the Doctrine of the Faith when in a letter to the US Bishops in 1973, it said

---

2. Once again, the issue is not the divine law of indissolubility, but the human laws and legal processes we use for determining whether an indissoluble marriage actually exists in a given case.

> In regard to admission to the sacraments, Ordinaries are asked on the one hand to stress observance of current discipline and, on the other hand, encourage pastors to exercise special care in seeking out those who are living in an irregular union by applying, in addition to other right means, the Church's approved practice in the internal forum (April 11, 1973).

In response to a request for further clarification, the Secretary of the Congregation said, in 1975

> I would like to state now that this phrase must be understood in the context of traditional moral theology. These couples may be allowed to receive the sacraments on two conditions: that they try to live according to the demands of Christian moral principles and that they receive the sacraments in churches in which they are not known so that they will not create any scandal.

There are other distinctions that also need to be made:

> Pastors must know that, for the sake of truth, they are obliged to exercise careful discernment of situations. There is in fact a difference between those who have sincerely tried to save their first marriage and have been unjustly abandoned, and those who through grave fault have destroyed a canonically valid marriage. Finally, there are those who have entered into a second union for the sake of the children's upbringing, and who are sometimes subjectively certain in conscience that their previous and irreparably destroyed marriage had never been valid (*FC* 84).

These distinctions would be superfluous if there were to be only one and the same solution for all. Canon lawyers and theologians find it necessary to distinguish between (a) 'conflict situations' (when the internal and external forum are in conflict because there is serious reason to believe that a previous marriage was invalid but its invalidity cannot be proved in the external forum); and (b) 'hardship situations' in which the previous marriage is presumed to have been valid.[3]

---

3. This distinction was made by Ladislas Orsy in a noteable issue of *Jurist*, 30 (1970), *Intolerable Marriage Situations, Conflict between External and Internal Forum.*

Catholics who believe there could be serious grounds to question the validity of their marriage should not underestimate the value of taking their case to the Matrimonial Tribunal. There are some who feel daunted by this prospect (partly because of obsolete information). For some it seems genuinely beyond their ability. There are others who appreciate the Tribunal process knowing that their situation will be objectively and professionally examined, and they hope in this way to more effectively reach closure. Many find the process positively healing.

It can happen, however, that sometimes the grounds on which a previous marriage is believed to be invalid cannot be proved in the external forum of the Matrimonial Tribunal. When such cases are dealt with in the internal forum, this can result in a decision to receive the sacraments of Penance and Holy Communion while continuing in the new relationship. The decision reached 'in conscience' or 'in the internal forum' (together with sorrow for any previous guilt there may have been and openness to any future possibility of convalidation in the external forum), is sufficient basis for resuming a full sacramental life.

> In an internal forum solution, a person makes a decision that it is appropriate to receive Communion, even though the irregular marital situation cannot be regularised in the external forum. It is not a question of a confessor, pastor, or other priest giving permission to receive Communion. No priest has authority to do this. However, a priest may assist the person in forming his/her conscience, e.g. that the previous marriage was invalid, and it is impossible to prove this in the external forum, and that consequently the present union is not adulterous. (WH Woestmann, *Sacraments of Initiation, Penance, Anointing of the Sick,* Ottawa, Faculty of Canon Law, 1992, 135.)

Sometimes it is said that such second marriages are 'valid in conscience'. This phrase risks confusing the juridic order (which deals with validity) and the moral order (which deals with right and wrong). In the judiric order, the first marriage is presumed valid until the contrary is proved (c 1060). This is also why decisions reached in the internal forum cannot result in the second marriage being celebrated canonically in the external forum.[4]

Recent developments in the jurisprudence of Matrimonial Tribunals allow that even when the facts of a case cannot be corroborated in the usual way, moral certainty concerning nullity can sometimes, nevertheless, be attained based on solid attestation of the petitioner's integrity. This means that when a marriage really is invalid, its invalidity is less likely to remain 'unprovable'.[5] A wider range of grounds for nullity has also been recognised.

Even so, there are also *subjective factors* that can prevent resolution through the Tribunal process. Hurt and confusion, fear, inherited prejudice, and just the struggles of coping can put the Tribunal process out of some people's reach. Our tradition speaks of 'moral impossibility'. It is too theoretical to speak only of how much the *Tribunal* can now achieve. It is also a matter of how much the *people* can manage, and a matter of what the Church will do for those who are today's 'lame, blind and deaf'.

The greater difficulty is with the 'hardship situations' in which there is no reason to suspect the invalidity of the first marriage. The clarification given to the US bishops by the Congregation (quoted above) spoke of couples being 'allowed to receive the sacraments on two conditions, that they try to live according to the demands of Christian moral principles,

4. Some argue, however, that Catholics caught in a genuine conflict situation can marry in a non-canonical way:
   It is not subversive of Church authority to hold that a person's right to marry (so clearly taught by the Church herself) may override the duty to comply with positive (man-made) law, even Church law. Such a person is free in conscience to contract marriage under whatever form it is available. (W Daniel SJ, 'On Marriage and Divorce', in *Compass Theology Review*, Summer 1986: 36; cf also Himes and Coriden, 'Pastoral Care of the Divorced and Remarried', in *Theological Studies*, March 1996: 99)
5. Prior to these developments, some authors were exploring other ways of determining whether an applicant's conviction concerning the invalidity of the first marriage could be given recognition in the external forum. L Orsy recalls the medieval practice of Tribunals of Conscience, and asks 'could the Church revive and enlarge an old tradition and institute Tribunals of Conscience for deserving cases that do not fall within the boundaries of our laws?' ('The Function of Ecclesial Decision: A Theological Evaluation of Marriage Tribunals', in *Concilium*, September 1973: 45; see also W Basset, 'The Role of the Local Bishop in the Sacrament of Marriage', in *Concilium*, September 1973: 47–60).

and that they receive the sacraments in churches in which they are not known so that they will not create any scandal'. The first condition echoes traditional teaching that what is required of penitents in order to receive the Sacrament of Penance is not certainty that they will succeed in avoiding wrong-doing, but that they will '*try to live* according to the demands of Christian moral principles. . . '—even if it is foreseen that they will not always succeed (emphasis mine).

Pope John Paul II recognised that succeeding can take time, and spoke of the 'law of gradualness' (*FC* 34). This does not mean that the law itself applies less to some and more to others, or less at some times and more at others. It simply acknowledges that individuals' subjective dispositions and abilities need time to strengthen and that this reality must be respected.

This law of gradualness is the reason why there is no inconsistency in asking people to align their lives to objective truth, *and* celebrating the Sacrament of Penance with them when they sincerely are trying to do that, but are not yet able to do so fully. This is not an *exception* to the normal requirements for receiving the Sacraments of Penance and Holy Communion. It *is* the normal requirement.

It is also according to our moral tradition not to ask of couples more than they are capable of. Even when Jesus was referring to situations that exclude re-marriage, he acknowledged that not everyone is capable of being a 'eunuch' for the sake of the kingdom, that is, of forgoing marriage for the sake of witnessing to how it was 'in the beginning' (cf Matt 19:1–12).

The second condition mentioned by the Congregation was that when couples in such second marriages receive Holy Communion it should be in circumstances that do not cause scandal. This is usually taken to mean in places where their circumstances are not known. But there is more than one way of avoiding scandal. The more neglected way, and less patronising way, is to educate the Catholic community concerning the Church's 'approved practices'. Good catechesis concerning Tribunal practice, and a correct understanding of what is meant by the 'internal forum solution' would enable the Catholic people to understand that when they see others who are in a second marriage going to Holy Communion, there may be good reason for not presuming that they are 'living in sin', or that there has been a change in the Church's teaching on indissolubility. For the same reasons, it cannot be presumed that their actions are 'giving scandal', that is, leading others into sin or causing them spiritual harm.

This makes it necessary to examine the reasons for excluding divorced-remarried Catholics from Holy Communion. There are two reasons, and they are both valid. The question is whether they apply *in all circumstances*. One reason is given in c 915 which says that those 'who obstinately persist in manifest grave sin' are to be excluded. Even if it is claimed that that phrase refers to an objective situation, it is nevertheless the language that properly speaking describes the subjective state of a bad conscience. But that is what cannot always be presumed. And as often as it can be doubted whether a Catholic in an irregular marriage coming up for Holy Communion is 'obstinately persisting in manifest serious sin', c 18 and cc 213, 843/1 and 912 apply, and so Holy Communion should not be refused.

It is because of this that official teaching no longer bases the exclusion on the assumption that such people are manifestly persisting in grave sin. And so instead—this is the second reason—it refers to an 'objective contradiction' between their life and the Lord's teaching; this is what excludes them from sharing the sacrament of unity. Again, the point is correct, but some would say *not absolute* given the Church's practice of allowing non-Catholics in some situations to receive Holy Communion notwithstanding their lack of full communion.

It is *a general authorisation* to allow Catholics in these situations to receive the Sacrament that is not acceptable, because that comes too close to a de facto acceptance of civil marriage as an alternative to maintaining the indissolubility of marriage.[6]

6. Although the three German bishops' proposal was intended to address individual situations, it seems they would have allowed the same solution for those whose first marriages were presumably valid (hardship cases) as for those whose first marriage may not have been valid (conflict cases).

The letter from the Congregation for the Doctrine of the Faith, October 1994, refers to the various 'new pastoral proposals' and responds that 'a new union cannot be recognised as valid if the preceding marriage was valid', which, of course, is not necessarily the case in conflict situations. The letter also asserts that the practice of 'not admitting the divorced and remarried to Holy Communion' has been the Church's 'constant and universal practice'. It needs to be recalled, however, that the Council of Trent deliberately avoided condemning the Eastern practice of *oikonomia*, which does allow for a sacramental life (cf P Fransen, 'Divorce on the Grounds of Adultery–the Council of Trent', in *Concilium*, May 1970: 89 ff), though the Roman Catholic Church has never endorsed the Eastern practice.

Letter Twenty

Male & Female God Made Them

Dear Joan,

You have shared with me the deep hurt you feel over ways women have been treated in society and in the Church, and told me of your affection for your fifteenth century namesake, Joan of Arc, who suffered at the hands of Church and state, and who is now recognised as a martyr and saint.

You also asked how I see the road ahead to full recognition of women's rights. I shall limit myself to reflecting on the distinctive contribution Judeo Christian revelation can make to that journey, and why it may well be decisive for reaching the goal.

I think an essential pre-requisite for progress is unpatronising compassion. I mean the ability to suffer with those who suffer. Without compassion, we will not find within ourselves the passion needed for uprooting entrenched cultural assumptions that tend to 'justify' domination and inequality. Compassion needs to be second nature to us, which is not made any easier by our constant exposure to brutality in its many forms, including violence presented as entertainment. Our culture de-sensitises us to what is in fact evil. Judeo Christian revelation is uniquely counter-cultural to this because it reveals a God of compassion and draws us into compassionate loving—suffering with those who suffer.

Our need to listen

In his first Encyclical letter, Pope John Paul II reminded us that a deeper understanding of history leads to a deeper understanding of the mystery of Christ; The Redeemer of Mankind (*Redemptor Hominis*, 1979) (RH)

13, and therefore of God's purposes. This implies that there are moments when the human race reaches new levels of awareness, often in hindsight, when we see what we had not previously seen so clearly.

After describing the lack of good judgement of those he called 'prophets of gloom', who 'behaved as though they had learned nothing from history', Pope John XXIII said

> In the present order of things, divine providence is leading us to a new order of human relations, which by our human efforts and even beyond our human expectations, are directed towards the fulfilment of God's greater and inscrutable designs. (Opening Address at the Second Vatican Council)

We also speak of 'signs of the times'. The changes that take place in the world are not themselves 'signs of the times' in a theological sense. The signs to which we look for indications of God's purposes are the longings, expectations, hopes and questionings that emerge from the changes. The Church's social teaching refers often to people's aspirations for equality, for participation in the decisions that affect them, for self-determination, and for a more humane world. The Church's appeal to these aspirations is based on its own conviction that to know people's deepest and truest aspirations is to know something of what God is wanting to tell us. Even the fact that these aspirations are sometimes misinterpreted does not change the fact that the aspirations themselves may be authentic (see Pope Paul VI, The Eightieth Anniversary of *Rerum Novorum*, 1971, *Octogesimo Adveniens*, n 30).

In his Encyclical letter Peace on Earth (*Pacem in Terris*, 1963), the same Pope had named the aspirations of women to participate in the decisions that affect them and affect society as one of the signs of the times (n 41).

Because even authentic human aspirations can be misinterpreted, the Church

> has always had the duty of scrutinising the signs of the times and interpreting them in the light of the gospel, and must do this in order to carry out its task (Pastoral Constitution on the Church in the Modern World, *Gaudium et Spes*,) (GS) n 4.

There are two moments in this task of scrutinising and interpreting: first there needs to be adequate social research—listening; and then theological reflection on the findings.

The kind of theological reflection needed requires that we be 'transformed by the renewal of our mind so that we may know what is the will of God' (Rom 12:2);—our own deeper conversion. Merely drawing conclusions from general principles hardly requires the kind of 'transformation' St Paul was speaking about. The kind of theological reflection required is more of the nature of spiritual discernment. This does not stop at our own reactions and 'how we feel' about what is said; rather, it notices those deeper movements of peace or disquiet or challenge or joy that run like the deep current below the surface of consciousness, where we are being 'drawn by the Father' (cf Jn 6:44) and 'prompted by the Holy Spirit' (cf Rom 8:14, Gal 5:16-25).

When we listen to the stories and perceptions of women who have been living their faith and who are either still trying or have given up, we are in a certain sense making their experience our own, as the Pastoral Constitution on the Church in the Modern World enjoins us to do (n 1). It involves a way of listening that wants to know more than whether their views are right or wrong. That judgement can also be necessary, but it is not enough. Even poorly expressed opinions can be used by God as catalysts for indicating how God wants us to respond. In this sense, every opinion is relevant—which is not to say every opinion is 'valid'.

Listening to those who experience the stress of wondering whether to stay with the Church out of loyalty and to share responsibility for its future, or instead move out for the sake of personally coping better and not becoming more alienated, we begin to understand their real pain and their anger. We begin to experience unpatronising compassion and commitment to the cause.

In recent years, much of that pain and anger has been dissipated through the greater involvement of women in the decision-making processes of pastoral and administrative planning at parish and diocesan levels. But there is still a clumsy, non-empathetic, business-as-usual streak in a small minority of clerics that makes this listening an on-going necessity.[1]

Why we call it sin

Like you, I believe that advancing right relationships between people, and especially between men and women, is at the heart of renewal—both for the Church and for society. It could hardly be otherwise because it is related to sin and redemption. Again, Judeo Christian revelation helps us to see what we are dealing with.

Those who have gone soft on the idea of sin, or who make it meaningless by relativising it, put themselves at a loss for finding any in-depth explanation of the domination of women by men. After all, most of it takes place within the law (which struggles even to deal with the worst of it). Nor can culture explain it: cultures transmit and perpetuate it, but if we are to have a reason for changing what is rotten within any given culture we need to establish that it comes back to choices people make. Judeo Christian revelation puts the domination of women by men squarely at the door of sinful choices—attributed to Adam and Eve in the mythological narrative used by the Book of Genesis to tell us how things were 'in the beginning', ie God's original purpose. It points to the distortion of human relationships, and especially the domination of women by men, as sin's most immediate consequences. It is said to the woman: 'your desire shall be for your husband and he shall rule over you' (Gen 3:16). It is worse for the man because the perpetrator of evil is more diminished by it than is the victim.

In this distortion of the relationship between male and female, it is human nature itself that is distorted because it was as male and female we were made *human* (Gen 1:27).

Redemption is about the undoing of sin and its consequences, and restoring us to how it was 'in the beginning'. So what was God's original purpose for us? What does it mean to have been made in the image and likeness of God (Gen 1:27)? Creation exists because God chose to create.

1. Samples of what women expressed during research conducted for New Zealand's Catholic Commission for Justice, Peace and Development (1990) are provided in Appendix II).

Our own existence was not owed to us—it is entirely *gift*. Consequently, we are true to our own nature by *being gifts*—by being '*for others*'.[2]

It was in freely giving his life for us that Jesus turned sin around on itself, restoring God's original plan. The early Christian hymn recorded in Philippians 2:16 ff gives us a reverse image of the kind of autonomy Adam and Eve wanted, in the Genesis story.

In the language of the Letter to the Ephesians, 5:21-33, Jesus gave his life for his bride the Church. The original readers of that letter were used to the idea of man being the 'head' of the wife. The author picks up the image they were used to, and gives it a whole new meaning. Christian husbands can only be head in the manner of Christ who sacrificed himself for his bride the Church. This is the radical renewal that the Gospel brings to human relationships at the very heart of what it means to be human, namely male and female. Their 'subjection' to each other is to be carried out in a way that reflects their 'reverence for Christ' and is to be mutual (Eph 5:21). Each puts the other first; each is *for the other.*

In this new way of being—'in Christ'—the original dignity and equality of male and female are restored. Neither is preferred above the other—there is 'no more male or female' in the way that culture had transmitted the inherited distortion (Gal 3:28).

This sure basis for the absolutely equal dignity of male and female is based on what we have become and *are*—in Christ. Contemporary Western culture focuses more on what we *do* than on what we *are*. When it comes to reflecting on male and female, the focus on *doing* leads to showing how much they are the same. Differentiations are even perceived as somehow threatening to equality. On the other hand, reflection at the deeper level of *being* rather than *doing* enables us to value and affirm the differences, the gifts and the originality of each. There is no need for either to prove himself or herself by taking on the characteristics of the other in order to establish equality. Equal dignity is already established by what they *are*—in God's original plan, restored by Christ.

---

2. This is how the Judeo Christian scriptures show us to ourselves, but deep down we already seem to know it, which is why we spontaneously admire an unselfish life, and feel disgusted by a grasping, egocentric way of life.

The problem is in the time it takes all of us to open ourselves to God's plan and to union with Christ: again, our conversion. Clinging to the false securities of sin-infected cultural patterns and pressures, we are slow to open ourselves to the radical newness of the Gospel. Commenting on St Paul's saying that 'in Christ Jesus there no more slave or freeman', John Paul II lamented:

> How many generations were needed for such a principle to be realised in the history of humanity through the abolition of slavery! And what is one to say of the many forms of slavery to which individuals and peoples are subjected, which have not yet disappeared from history? (Apostolic Letter on the Dignity and Vocation of Women (*Mulieris Dignitatem*), Vatican Press, 1988 (MD), 24.

He had been saying that the subjection of husbands and wives to each other 'out of reverence for Christ' is not yet fully established 'in hearts, in consciences, behaviour and customs' both within marriage and 'in regard to women in every situation' (n 24).

The Letter to the Ephesians also makes use of the male female imagery to depict the relationship between Christ and all those for whom Christ gave his life (5:31-32). The image carries over to the celebration of Eucharist where Christ's self-giving is re-enacted and where we are invited to union with him in reciprocating love.

The author of Ephesians could well have added that just as Christian husbands are 'head' of their wives (in the imagery of his day) only insofar as they resemble Christ's self-giving, so too those who are called to symbolise Christ the head of His body can credibly do so only insofar as they resemble Christ the self-giving servant of all. Whatever about that, in the spousal imagery of Ephesians 5, womanhood has clearly been chosen to symbolise the paramount vocation of all of us—the vocation that precedes and undergirds every particular Christian calling.

Back to Joan of Arc

It was the intervention of a Pope that eventually vindicated St Joan of Arc and reversed her sham condemnation, and other Popes who beatified and canonised her. It saddens me that Pope John Paul II's intervention on behalf of the Dignity and Vocation of Women has too often been read through the lenses of contemporary Western ideologies, and not through the eyes of Judeo Christian revelation.

By entering more deeply into revealed truth about what it means to be human, we re-discover how it was 'in the beginning' and how this is being restored—'in Christ'. From there we move to particular issues.

Letter Twenty-One

Renewal and the Sacrament of Reconciliation

Dear theologians and canon lawyers

Much more important things could be said about reconciliation in general, and the Sacrament of Reconciliation in particular, than I intend to say here. This reflection is limited to just the issue of general confession and absolution.

(i) Fundamental principles

Jesus gave his Church authority to forgive sin, and to determine how best to do this. No sacrament has undergone more change down the centuries than the sacrament of Penance. And, of course, what has changed, can change again.

Whatever sacramental practices and laws the Church puts in place, they must ultimately be measured against needs of the Church's mission, which is always the higher law. The Church's mission is to be a sign of the mission of Christ:

> It was God who reconciled us to himself through Christ, and gave us the work of handing on this reconciliation (2 Cor 5:7–20).

In Christ, it is above all the abundance and gratuitousness of God's mercy that are revealed. And so to be faithful to its mission of 'handing on' this reconciliation, the Church's own practices must witness to the lavishness of God's forgiveness.[1]

1. This was the point of my own and others' interventions at the 1983 Synod on Reconciliation and Penance. (See *Origins*, 1983, 340–341).

(ii) The Church's tradition

The lavishness of God's mercy is put in relief in the practice of general confession and absolution. From the eighth to the twelfth century in the Latin Church, general confession and absolution, even for the forgiveness of serious sins, was practised in many different situations, and the accompanying prayers indicate that these rituals were often sacramental in the strict sense.[2]

From the fourth to the ninth century in the Eastern Churches, general confession and absolution were the only way (other than the discipline of public penance) that lay people could celebrate the Sacrament of Reconciliation for the forgiveness even of serious sins. Even today, the Eastern Churches celebrate general confession and absolution with greater frequency than does the Latin Church.

The Council of Trent taught the need for individual and integral confession of grave sins. But as the Council itself affirmed on several occasions, its teaching was limited to condemning errors taught by the Protestant Reformers, who had denied the need for individual confession to a priest. The foremost historian dealing with that time, Hubert Jedin has stated:

> The Council of Trent did not condemn in any way the thesis according to which absolution may be given in a global fashion following a general confession of guilt (see *La Maison Dieu*, 1970, 114).

(iii) The 1983 Synod

During the 1983 Synod there were widespread calls for an extended use of the third form of celebrating the Sacrament of Reconciliation.[3] Commentators generally agree that the post-conciliar Apostolic Exhortation on Penance and Reconciliation focuses more on private and individual reconciliation, whereas the Council[4] and the 1973 *Rite of Penance* fo-

---

2. It seems that already at that time, however, a general willingness to confess one's grave sins individually was an implied duty.
3. In notes I wrote during the Synod, I recorded that these calls kept coming even after we had been reminded of the restrictions imposed by the Code of Canon Law.
4. See Dogmatic Constitution on the Church, *Lumen Gentium*, 1963 (*LG*) 11; Decree on

cus more on the social and ecclesial nature and effects of sacramental reconciliation,[5] and communal celebrations of liturgical rites (*SC* 26, 27).

Pope John Paul II felt very conscious of our living in a culture that had lost its sense of sin and of God. He also felt it was necessary to emphasise that it is persons who sin, not the systems that might influence them. So too, it is persons who can change the systems and the institutions.[6] He was also concerned that wider use of the third form of celebrating the sacrament would further jeopardise the celebration of individual confession.[7]

(iv) Sensus Fidelium

It is to the whole body of the faithful that God gives a sure sense of what ultimately the faith means.[8] It belongs to those with teaching authority in the Church to authentically interpret the faith. Yet, they too, must learn the faith from the whole body of the faithful down the centuries. The Second Vatican Council taught that the Tradition (that is, the faith as expressed in the lives, beliefs and devotion of the faithful), the Scriptures, and the Church's teaching authority are 'so linked that one cannot stand without the others' (*Revelation* 10). There can be no teaching without listening.

During the Synod, bishops who asked that the third form of celebrating the sacrament be extended, or at least not further restricted, spoke of the profoundly moving and devout celebrations of God's presence and forgiveness that they themselves, some of their priests, and their people, had experienced where the third rite had been celebrated according the 1973 Rite of Penance. There is a theological basis for this deeper experi-

---

the Ministry and Life of Priests, *Presbyterorum Ordinis*, 1965 (*PO*) 5; *SC* 72.

5. See James Dallen, *Reconciliatio et Paenitentia, The Post Synodal Apostolic Exhortation*, in *Worship*, 1985, 98 ff).
6. 'Structures of sin are rooted in personal sin and thus always linked to the concrete acts of individuals who introduce them and make them difficult to remove' (John Paul II, The Social Concern of the Church, 1987, paragraph 35)
7. Historically, the demise of Rite I *preceded* the emergence of Rite III. Whether the wider acceptance of Rite III would hinder the *recovery* of Rite I or eventually restore it (but without the excesses and exaggerations that had become associated with it), is a different question. It is my recollection that the question of general confession and absolution was eventually not among the propositions put to the bishops for their vote at the Synod.
8. See *LG* 12, The Dogmatic Constitution on Divine Revelation (*Dei Verbum*), 1965 (*DV*) 10.

ence of reconciliation: it is because personal reconciliation in the sacrament is essentially an *ecclesial* event.

This same moving experience of God's presence and gift of forgiveness has been the experience of parishioners in a region of this diocese where for twelve years the third form of the sacrament was celebrated during Advent and Lent. These celebrations followed the 1973 Rite, and appropriate catechesis was given on the need for grave sins to be brought to individual confession. Opportunities for Rites I and II also continued to be offered. Many hundreds of parishioners from parishes in the region joined these celebrations.

Nevertheless, I felt it was my duty to disallow *pre-arranged* celebrations of the Third Rite. (I have always allowed general confession and absolution where bona fide arrangements have been made for Rite II, which has then turned out to be unmanageable in the circumstances. This will occur more frequently as priests become fewer. In such cases, I believe it would cause grave harm to send people away without the absolution for which, in good faith, they had come and to which they can be entitled—cf canons 213, 843/1).

My reason for intervening was not only out of respect for the *Motu Proprio Misericordia Dei* of April 2002, but also because individual confession and absolution better allow for some of the essential components of the conversion process.[9] Consequently, there would be too much to lose if

---

9.

- The key element of *sorrow* itself can be deepened and brought into sharper focus through the dialogue that takes place in rite 1 and through the experience of not being thought less of on account of what one has had to confess;
- The very act of *confessing* can make one focus more specifically on what one is being sorry for. Naming one's sins to another involves accepting the truth about one's self, all the more because it is being made known to another;
- In this 'moment of truth' one's sincere *purpose of amendment* is also revealed to another who is thereby being allowed to judge its sincerity before absolution is given.
- One's willingness to do *penance* is made explicit in the acceptance of a penance given by another who has been made aware of the sins for which the penance is being given.

All these are subtle and very human processes, but that is what 'grace builds on'. In fact, below a certain threshold, the absence of these elements would make absolution ineffective anyway. For example, if there wasn't a real commitment to breaking with serious sin. (Memorandum to Diocese, 2006).

general confession and absolution came to be regarded as a simple alternative to individual confession and absolution.

These are very good reasons for promoting Rites I and II. But how sure can we be that Rite III is in fact a threat to Rites I and II? Has the *sensus fidelium* been trying to say something that I, and others in authority, have not properly heard? What I have heard from other bishops during the Synod, and from those involved in this diocese, are not the voices of people who have lost their sense of sin, or of pastors who neglect to make Rites I and II available. They are the voices of people who recognise their sinfulness and want the sacrament, and the voices of sensitive, conscientious and loyal pastors.

For the priest who discontinued this practice at my insistence it is a matter of conscience:

> I now have to ask myself some questions. The call to do this was probably cemented by today's First Reading, the Second Thursday of Easter. As a pastor I have responsibility to feed the faith of the people entrusted to my pastoral care, so when four hundred to five hundred persons are not nourished by a faith celebration because of the word of men, even learned and holy men, what should I do? When the power of forgiveness, healing and reconciliation is not felt by that number of people to whom should I be faithful? When I hear the pain of men and women who have lived the faith for more than eighty years expressing their bewilderment at the Church's current discipline, with whom should I stand? When parishioners at the heart of the Parish, daily Mass goers, came and thanked me with tears in their eyes, for the opportunity to celebrate their faith in Rite Three, to whom should I listen?
>
> I originally thought that I would write my document and that by doing that I would be at peace, and I was for a while. Then I started to hear the stories, feel the pain, notice the bewilderment and hurt, and suddenly I knew the right to peace was not mine yet. I believe I have to push our Church leadership and then live with the restlessness that comes when one is challenging the powerful and more learned, and probably more faithful. I believe in the faith and goodness of these parishioners, I believe in their wisdom, I believe that they had made their choice twelve years ago regarding Rites One and Two, and I believe in the choice which they made to celebrate the Third Rite. I have to be faithful to them, faithful to the

> authority of the Church, but especially faithful to God. I am hearing Jesus' voice very strongly 'feed my sheep'.

Just before the Synod, the Professor of Canon Law at the Catholic University of America, Ladislas Orsy SJ had written:

> The falling away from the practice of confession may be partly due to the lack of a spirit of penance, but perhaps the people are rightly longing for other ways of receiving forgiveness for their ordinary weaknesses, other ways which can be easily brought forth from the treasury of the Church . . . Since the Church has known different ways of doing it in the past, there is no reason why new ways cannot be found today. (*America*, September 17, 1983, 127).
>
> . . . There is *no theological reason* why those who are not aware of 'sin to death' could not receive, even ordinarily, the sacrament in some other way (*ibid*) (emphasis mine).

(v) The Church's law

> Is there *any canonical reason* why 'those who are not aware of 'sin to death' could not receive, or even ordinarily, the sacrament in some other way?'

It is a firm principle of canon law that restrictions imposed by Church law are not to be extended beyond what the law itself specifically restricts (canon 18).

The canons governing general confession and absolution are of that kind: c 960 stipulates that individual confession and absolution are the only ordinary way of celebrating the Sacrament of Reconciliation for those who are *conscious of grave sin*. Even c 961's reference to those who would otherwise be deprived of Holy Communion for a lengthy period concerns those who are *conscious of grave sin*. The point to notice is that both canons concern those who are *conscious of grave sin*. The same is true of the *Motu Proprio Misericordia Dei*, which is explicitly intended to clarify and interpret the canons; it does not extend them.

Clearly we cannot approve practices that would contravene these canons. But what is to be said about making the sacrament available for those who, though conscious of their general sinfulness and need for the sacrament, are *not conscious of grave sin*? There are also those, for example in homes for the elderly and the mentally impaired, who are hardly able to commit grave sin. Even allowing for the value of individual confession and absolution when one's sins are not grave, this is not the situation envisaged by canons 960 and 961 and the *Motu Proprio*. It is *praeter legem*.

Even our insistence on the need for individual confession for grave sin must be tempered by what the Church has always taught concerning 'moral impossibility'. For some, the burden of individual confession is just 'too difficult'—at least at given times or circumstances in their lives.

Are we to ignore the pleas of those parents whose adolescent children, remarkably, are willing to be with them at celebrations involving general confession and absolution but seem unable to cope with Rites I and II? Is this not, in their regard, a matter of 'grave necessity'—if the alternative is that they will have no contact with the sacrament at all? These questions deserve further attention.

(iv) Praeter legem

Canons 960 and 961 and the *Motu Proprio Misericordia Dei* concern those who are conscious of grave sin and who are able to avail themselves of opportunities for individual confession. For them, general confession and absolution are not sufficient, and are not to be regarded as an ordinary way of celebrating the sacrament.

However, on the basis of canon 18, we cannot extend the meaning of these canons to disadvantage parishioners who *either are not conscious of grave sin, or though conscious of grave sins are not easily able to 'go to confession' due to physical or moral impossibility.*

These qualifying circumstances involve subjective factors, which ultimately only the penitents themselves can judge. *Our* responsibility is to (i) provide appropriate catechesis to help parishioners make informed judgements based on the teaching of the Church; (ii) help them deepen their appreciation of individual confession and absolution, preferably in a communal setting and (iii) make the sacrament as available as possible.

Letter Twenty-Two

'More Catholic than the Pope'

Dear Brendan,

You do well to speak up for the Church's teaching on sexual morality, and more of the lay faithful should do so—provided they do so accurately. Just as it can be misleading and harmful to reduce the Church's teachings to less than they mean, so too it can be misleading and harmful to inflate the Church's teachings to more than they mean—especially in matters of conscience.

When a national newspaper likens the Catholic Church to a Flat Earth Society because the Church questions the merits of condoms in preventing the spread of AIDS, it is in part because of the simplistic assumption that in ethical matters the end justifies the means. However, some responsibility for this reaction to the Church must lie with those members of the Church who exaggerate its teaching.

In recent years, when some theologians and bishops tried to correct this way of over-interpreting the Church's teaching, other members of the faithful, well meaning but less well informed, have accused them of trying to change the Church's teaching, or to allow 'exceptions' to the Church's teaching.

The question about whether in some circumstances it is permissible to use condoms is not a question about whether there can be 'exceptions' to the Church's teaching; not even exceptions in special circumstances. Rather, it is about circumstances that fall *outside the Church's teaching on contraception.*

The Church's teaching that contraception is wrong concerns sexual intercourse freely entered into between husband and wife. Its teaching on contraception is not about sexual activity outside of marriage (or even forced intercourse inside marriage). One only has to read the Encyclical *On the Regulation of Birth* (*Humanae Vitae*, 1968 (*HV*) properly to see that. Sexual intercourse outside of marriage is wrong, but the use of condoms in that context is a different ethical question. For example, when contraceptive medication is taken by people in danger of being raped, we are not dealing with *exceptions* to the Church's teaching, but with situations that fall *outside* the Church's teaching on contraception. That is why the Holy See itself, in the 1960s, was able to confirm that it was ethical for nuns living in fear of being raped (in the Congo) to take contraceptive measures. There was no marriage being contracepted.

When the Church discourages the use of condoms as a means of preventing AIDS, it is not because of their contraceptive effect, it is because their easy acceptance diminishes the incentive for self-restraint or chastity, and in this way *increases* the risk of promiscuity and the spread of AIDS. But when self-restraint is just not going to happen, then condoms might only be a last line of defence against infection.

Even in the case of consensual intercourse inside of marriage: when the intention is really to prevent a serious infection, the contraceptive effect is a side-effect, that is, not the directly intended effect, which for a sufficiently serious reason can be *allowed* to happen. This is an application of traditional moral principles which are recognised as part of the Church's teaching. It is not an exception to the Church's teaching.

If these matters appear to be 'exceptions', it is because the focus has been too simplistically on condoms, instead of on marriage. A blanket condemnation of condoms—regardless of whether the contracepting of a marriage is even involved—has led to an inflation of the Church's teaching that is ultimately unfaithful to the Catholic moral tradition and to *Humanae Vitae* itself. When some moral theologians, and individual members of the universal episcopate (for example, Cardinals Danneels and Martini) have opposed this inflation of the Church's teaching, they have not received the support they were entitled to receive from the universal episcopate which shares responsibility for Catholic orthodoxy.

Letter Twenty-Three

Where the Spirit Moves

Dear pastoral planners

Throughout salvation history, it is the Spirit of God that gives life and form where otherwise there is only void, chaos, desert and dry bones; (cf Gen 1:12; Deut 32:10,11; Is 43:19; Ezech 37:1–14). This Source of life is also the source of new life—as at the beginning of Jesus' ministry, and at the beginning of the Church's mission, and ever since. So, in looking for openings to renewal we need to look for signs of where the Spirit is already giving new life.

These are not difficult to see, or to interpret. Each year, tens of thousands of young people are attracted to Taize and other places of pilgrimage in search of contemplative and community prayer and ways of working for international justice and peace. Many are attracted to join the various New Ecclesial Movements, wanting to experience Christian community, support one another in living the gospel, and joyously witness to it; to pray together the Prayer of the Church, and spend time before the Blessed Sacrament; to offer hospitality, and reach out to people in need. All this is counter-cultural and indicative of where the Spirit of God is moving. By their fruits . . .

Within the parishes too, there are those who come together in faith-sharing groups, for scripture-based prayer, retreats in daily life, and for the experience of closer, more inclusive relationships. There are those who work for the enrichment of marriage and family life, and those who meet to reflect on their social and economic environment in the light of the gospel, and then act to bring about needed changes; (remember 'see, judge, act'?). On a broader front, there are Catholics—both young and retired—who are volunteering for periods of service abroad on development projects.

The way the churches are packed for the major Christian feasts, even by Catholics who are not there every Sunday; the constant stream who come to daily Masses in parishes throughout the country (they are the stream that never dries up even in the severest drought); the constant return of congregations for communal celebrations of the sacrament of Penance especially in Advent and Lent; new-found devotion to the Cross, Icons and pilgrimages as in the lead-up to World Youth Day; and those parishioners who quietly get on with the works of mercy, as in the Society of St Vincent de Paul and the Young Vinnies—all these, too, are signs of where the Spirit is giving new life.

There are also programmes aimed not only at renewing discipleship but also enabling Christian people to make disciples of others. One such programme that is Christ-centred, community-centred, holistic, and has a proven record on all the continents and with all age groups, is Alpha. It involves the Christian churches working together, and since the 1970s has involved over 6 million people.

If renewal means being led by the Spirit, then the renewal of our parishes will take its cue from what these signs are saying to us. They are pointing to a desire for more intimate experiences of Christian community, but also a stronger desire to share it with others; the need for people to feel 'at home' in the Church; a felt need for simplicity, and for greater inclusiveness; opportunities to experience the mystery of God and contemplative prayer, and the need to make a difference in society. All these are 'openings to renewal'.

Before we focus on each of them, let us notice how it works: something happens to us through contact with people who do any of these things. We seem to know more surely that what they believe in is right. What we hope for seems more certain. Without the need for words, their choices quietly summon us to deeper faith and deeper conversion. Renewal is like a flame that is being passed around.

Now let us look at what the signs are saying. First and foremost, people's desire for 'opportunities to experience the mystery of God and contemplative prayer' means they will come to parishes and to liturgies where they can sense the presence of God. Otherwise, we need not expect them.

People's need to feel *at home in the Church*—their parish, their diocese, and the universal Church—means they need to feel they are at *their* place, not someone else's place. That is the point of inculturation.

Those, too, whose limited contact with their parish is around births, deaths and marriages—above all at these times—need to come away with lasting and *good memories*. These are archetypal times in anyone's life, and the memories go deep, for better or for worse.

Renewal needs to focus on *community*: it is sometimes said that in large urban conglomerations the traditional form of parish is not what best serves community, because community needs to be small enough for people to relate to each other easily. After allowing for special chaplaincies (cf Code of Canon Law, cc 516, 564) and for the special situation of migrants, refugees and iterant peoples for whom 'personal parishes' can be appropriate (cc 518, 568), it still remains that people see themselves primarily in terms of where they live and have their families. Their normal desire is to form communities of worship and service based on *family, home and neighbourhood*, rather than groupings related to work, study, and specialised interests. The emergence of small 'base' communities seems to be further confirmation of this.

It is understandable that the New Movements show more commitment to living the gospel and sharing it than is shown by most parishioners. Parishes include disparate groups, for example, minorities who are looking for a fuller commitment to Christian life than they are getting from the routines of parish life; smaller minorities who want to pull back from where they perceive the Church is going; and majorities who faithfully carry on, mainly content just to fulfil their obligations. Pastors have the difficult task of trying to bring them all along together.

This suggests the need for smaller cells or communities within parishes to provide for the deeper commitment some are seeking, and scope for these cells to act as catalysts for the life and mission of the whole parish.

As we move towards greater *collaboration between parishes* and better rationalisation of resources, we have found it necessary to ensure that parishes retain their own identity as centres of worship and apostolates. People do not have quite the same feeling of belonging to a cluster of parishes. But we also need to acknowledge that a congregation can be too small—either to experience the liturgy as it is meant to be experienced, or to carry out the apostolates that are part of the Church's life. Parishes of that size need to be amalgamated.

Renewal of the Church also needs to focus on *inclusiveness*. Jesus' preference for mixing with 'tax collectors and sinners' looms out at us on every page of the gospel. It should concern us greatly, therefore, that even some Catholics perceive the Church as being for the virtuous and respectable, and feel themselves unworthy and disqualified. They need to know that the Church is theirs too, that they belong, that their prayer counts, whatever their circumstances. We sing 'Come as You Are' which puts it very well. What do we do to pass on the invitation?

This is especially needed for Catholics whose circumstances prevent them from receiving Holy Communion. The Church cannot pretend that being at variance with Jesus' teaching regarding marriage does not matter or make any difference. We are *all* obliged to witness to his teaching. Even so, Catholics in those difficult circumstances are not separated from the Church, and when they take part in the Mass and other liturgies, their prayers are united with the prayer of Christ and the whole Church. They can be in communion with Christ even when this communion cannot be sacramentally expressed. Pope John Paul II encouraged all, including those who cannot receive Holy Communion, to experience the 'strength, consolation and support' he experienced when spending time before Christ in the Blessed Sacrament.

Consistent with the need to make these Catholics feel 'at home', there has developed a practice of coming forward to receive a blessing while others receive Holy Communion. Children who have not yet made their first Holy Communion sometimes do the same.[1]

1. It seems incredible that officials of the Congregation for Divine Worship and Discipline of the Sacraments would spend time examining whether this practice can be allowed; incredible that others would even ask, and that some even seem to hope this further 'change' will be forbidden! (reported in *Adoremus*, February 2009).

Inclusiveness also reaches out to today's 'outcasts'—those who experience society's fears and prejudices, for example those just released from prison, those in need of Women's Refuge, homosexuals, migrants, the mentally unstable, victims of war or famine.

The renewal of the Church depends absolutely on our parishes having more *youthful profiles*. This will not happen unless young people are given *lead roles* of one kind or another, and are *called to them by name*, not just as 'young persons'. Home is where each is called by his or her own name, and where each is given responsibilities. There can be no doubt that the Holy Spirit is moving powerfully among young people. This is meant to enrich the whole Church.

Earlier in these reflections, I spoke of the need for contemplative living, and of Pope John Paul II's exhortation to the New Zealand bishops to 'make a systematic effort in your dioceses and parishes to open new doors to the experience of Christian prayer and contemplation . . . ' This requires a renewed sense of what Sunday means.

> For Christians, Sunday is the 'fundamental feast day' established not only to mark the succession of time but to reveal time's meaning' (Pope John Paul II, Apostolic Letter On Keeping the Lord's Day Holy, *Dies Domini,* 1998, 2).
>
> Unfortunately, when Sunday loses its fundamental meaning and becomes merely part of a 'weekend', it can happen that people stay locked within a horizon so limited that they can no longer see 'the heavens' (4).
>
> Since Sunday is the weekly Easter, recalling and making present the day upon which Christ rose from the dead, it is also the day which reveals the meaning of time. It has nothing in common with the cosmic cycles according to which natural religion and human culture tend to impose a structure on time, succumbing perhaps to the myth of eternal return.
>
> The Christian Sunday is wholly other! Springing from the Resurrection, it cuts through human time, the months, the years, the centuries, like a directional arrow which points them towards their target: Christ's Second Coming. Sunday foreshadows the last day,

> the day of the Parousia, which in a way is already anticipated by Christ's glory in the event of the Resurrection.
>
> If Sunday is a day of joy, Christians should declare by their actual behaviour that we cannot be happy 'on our own'. They look around to find people who may need their help. It may be that in their neighbourhood or among those they know there are sick people, elderly people, children or immigrants who precisely on Sundays feel more keenly their isolation, needs and suffering (72).

It is not enough to think of the Sunday 'Mass obligation'. The Mass celebrates what the Sunday means.

In a community that celebrates the Eucharist, whatever its shape or form or size, the 'mystery of faith' is fully present. 'The mystery is Christ among you, your hope of glory' (Col 1:27).

I have met him there. So have we all, and been renewed.

Epilogue

In the community called Christian,
I find people of flesh and blood and ordinary lives
living in expectation of meeting You,
undefeated by their personal failures and by death itself.
I have watched their faces in quiet prayer
and in songs of joy;
I have heard their professions of faith
and confessions of failure;
I have felt humbled no less by their repentance than
by their faithfulness;
I have known their sacrifices,
been empowered by their serenity
and learned the reason for the hope that is in them.
Their sureness is not based on any success of their own
but on what they believe You have done for them.

There is power in what they seem to know,
the more because human nature is weak.
I thank you Father, for having revealed great things
to little ones.
In the community of those who live
now not they but Christ living in them,
I have seen frail human nature raised up
reaching heights of hope and depths of peace
which nothing in the world could give, nor take away. IN THEIR MIDST
I COME TO KNOW
THAT HE who enabled the lame to walk
and the blind to see
and sinners to start again

IS RISEN,
for that is what their lives proclaim.
And so I believe in him
in whom they have placed their trust.

(*I Believe within the Church*, P J Cullinane, [Dublin: Veritas, 2006], 20–21)

Appendix I

Post-conciliar and semi-official clarifications

The period of implementing the Council's teachings brought forth further official and semi-official clarifications:

> [The main altar] should be free-standing to allow the ministers to walk around it easily and Mass to be celebrated facing the people, which is desirable whenever possible. The altar should occupy a place that it truly is the centre on which the attention of the whole congregation of the faithful naturally focuses . . . (General Instruction of the Roman Missal, (*GIRM*) 299).

> The dignity of the Word of God requires the church to have a place that is suitable for the proclamation of the Word and is *a natural focus* for the people during the Liturgy of the Word (309).

> The priest-celebrant's chair ought to stand as a symbol of his office of presiding over the assembly and of directing prayer . . . (310).

> The place in a church or oratory where the Eucharist is reserved in a tabernacle should be truly a place of honour. It should also be suited to private prayer so that the faithful may readily and to their advantage continue to honour the Lord in this sacrament by private worship. Therefore, it is recommended that as far as possible the tabernacle be placed in a chapel set apart from the main body of the church, especially in churches where frequently there are marriages and funerals and in places that, because of their artistic or historical treasures, are visited by many people (CDWS, Instruction on Worship of the Eucharist, 1967, 53).

> It is preferable that the tabernacle be located, according to the judgement of the diocesan bishop, either in the sanctuary apart from the altar of celebration..., or in some chapel suitable for the

faithful's private adoration and prayer and which is organically connected to the church and readily visible to the Christian faithful (*GIRM*, n 315).

In relation to the design of each church, the music group should be so placed that its character as truly a part of the gathered community of the faithful with a special function to carry out stands out clearly. The location should also assist the choir to exercise it's function . . . (312).

The reorganisation of existing churches and the planning of new churches must be seen as part of the liturgical renewal which is not limited merely to the changing of rites and texts. Similarly, the renewal of church architecture should not be limited to changes in design and construction but should be *part of a larger programme whose aim is to foster the formation of the faithful* (Episcopal Liturgical Commission of Ireland, 1972, *Building and Reorganisation*, Dublin: Veritas Publications, n 1.3).

The architectural character of existing churches and of any existing works of art of genuine merit should be retained, but only insofar as may be consistent with the spirit of the liturgy (*Ibid*, n 1.14).

Appendix II

See Letter 20, Footnote 1

'I stay in the Church with difficulty, but I stay because I have, through Baptism, both a right to be there, and a share of responsibility for the quality of the Church's life…' (*Made in God's Image*, C Cheyne, Report prepared for Catholic Commission Justice, Peace & Development, February 1990, page 111).

'I have wept with pain while sitting in a Church listening to scripture aimed at men, praying for men and to a male deity; singing about men, while three-quarters of the congregation are women. What offends me even more is that women accept their invisibility and have little concept of their value as persons—we have been colonised.' (p 110).

'I live largely on the edge of parish life at present, content with prayer and sacrament. I know that growth towards wholeness is possible, painful, but worthwhile. For me that growth meant questioning authority and loyalty to traditional Church. I suspect there are a number of women in the Church, especially married women, who would like to grow in their faith but are frightened of the consequences—I see and hear them in groups, at retreats, etc.' (p 111).

'At the end of the twentieth century we are a cultural milieu where, without reference to Christ or his Church, the secular world under the guidance of the Holy Spirit, is painfully accepting this truth (the equality of all people) and taking steps to implement it. In such a cultural environment, the gap between its theology and its practice is making the Church appear fundamentally illogical if not dishonest in the eyes of many of its members, especially women. We have to record our sadness and dismay at the number of Catholic women, many of whom we would never have dreamed would ever give up the Church, who are quietly leaving it. Women's awareness of the injustices they suffer is gathering momentum with unforeseen rapidity and it is having a powerful impact on women in the Church. The women's movement, so called, is no longer the preserve of a comparatively few people and it is nothing short of ludicrous to suggest that this study is instigated by them. We live amongst working class women and we are amazed at the speed of change that is taking place in their attitudes to women's place in society. What was only a small landslide as recently as ten years ago is becoming an avalanche. It is not going to stop because it is unstoppable.' (p 92–93)

'I believe we, as Church, are impoverished in our theology, our liturgy, our practices, by the historical fact that the development of all these areas has been (and is) exclusively in the hands of men. Until such time as women have an equal say in the major decision-making bodies of the Church, this impoverishment will remain. 'But we are complementary' says a female critic of your project—and that is precisely the point: there is no complementarity in the male power structure of the Church.' (p 93)

'There is a great anomaly in being responsible and taking charge of one's faith development which is what the Church demands of us as adult, and how it then copes with inquisitive, questioning and aware people in its community.' (p 96)

'In this diocese we have many highly qualified skilled and experienced hospital chaplains who are women religious. We get little or no respect, acknowledgement, remuneration or whatever from the 'official Church', especially the diocesan vicars who appoint retired clergy over our heads without consultation, etc. These men do untold harm and we have to calm the hurts they perpetrate while avoiding treading on their toes or we may be banned. We are highly regarded by staff, patients and relatives, especially by those who are marginalised by the attitude of the clergy past and present. I could give you shocking examples of the harm done by these insensitive, untrained and unsuitable priests in these positions.' (p 100)

'I found pregnancy difficult and have empathy with all pregnant women, but again I believe collectively as Church we fail to support women. Recently I was in the congregation (where)... the celebrant offered condolences to the young father and tagged his wife's name on. No acknowledgement was made of the fact that she had nurtured that life inside her own body for nine months and the special sense of physical, spiritual and emotional loss she was experiencing. Had the celebrant been a female, this omission could not have occurred… Pregnancy is a women's experience and no male can identify with it. So it is ignored…' (p 89)

'I became increasingly aware of how powerless ordinary parishioners, especially the women (who form the bulk of the active parishioners) are, and I personally as a woman religious, experienced painful, energy-sapping frustration and anger. No matter how excited, innovative or creative we became about aspects of parish life, in the final analysis, the priest whose perception of life and reality was masculine and essentially different from the feminine view of the most involved of his parishioners, had the power to say 'no'… and no one of us had any real recourse elsewhere… The parish priest is not accountable to anyone… I am not talking about individual priest, I am talking about a system which can allow so much power to one person, always a male.' (p101–102)

'The efforts that women religious have made, at considerable cost, to educate themselves theologically are rarely recognised in our Church, while a man who has not necessarily done anything beyond the level of the seminary, and that possibly limited and well out-of-date, automatically become a Doctor of Divinity.' (p 102).

'The language and rituals the Church uses are offensive to me. Many say that looking at language is a trivial matter, but to me it expresses a way of thinking. We have at our disposal a language which can be precise and inclusive and I feel strongly it should be used. I can no longer feel part of a community of worship when referred to as a brother.' (p 73).

Index

Subject